Liverpool Kingfisher

By

Dave F Cowhig

A True Story

Copyright © 2021 Dave Cowhig

ISBN: 978-1-7391835-0-9

All rights reserved, including the right to reproduce this book, or portions thereof in any form. No part of this text may be reproduced, transmitted, downloaded, decompiled, reverse engineered, or stored, in any form or introduced into any information storage and retrieval system, in any form or by any means, whether electronic or mechanical without the express written permission of the author.

To Pauline for all her help and patience

Dedicated to all the sailors of HMS Egret Sunk by enemy action 27th August 1943

Toxteth Liverpool 1981

The high-rise flat is poorly furnished but clean, the sitting room simple old furniture, two small bookshelves with a collection of French and Chinese books under a window that looked eighteen floors down onto a park. On the main wall was an ornate sideboard. Its legs intricately carved dragons' feet, and the centre door displayed a frieze of a kingfisher with its wings wide swooping down. The finish was black lacquer with gold inlays. Three framed photographs on top, two well-dressed young women, one European and one Chinese, sat at a table; a photo of an attractive middle-aged woman signed 'All my love Monique.', The third was a man in a British Army uniform. Sitting on the sideboard is a young Chinese girl dressed in poor clothes. An older woman sat next to a two-bar electric fire with a small blanket around her shoulders. The doorbell rang. Stiffly walking up the hall, she opened the door; the visitor in her early thirties was smartly dressed, carrying a briefcase. She showed her identification card.

'Hello, I'm from the hospital. Are you, Joanna Barlow?'

'Yes, that's me, but I didn't ask for a doctor. There must be some mistake.'

'I'm a social worker. My name is Rita Jones; I've come to see if you're alright. Can I come in? I have a form to fill in. It won't take long?'

'Well, as long as you'll be quick.' Joanna hesitated for a moment, then opened the door wide. 'Please sit down. I'd offer you a cup of tea, but I don't have any milk. The lifts are broken again; fine going down coming back up is a hike.' The Chinese girl on the sideboard speaks.

'I like her shoes; they nice.'

'Your shoes are nice Mai would love them.' Joanna said as she gazed down at them.

'I have a few forms for you to fill in. First, why did you leave the hospital?' Joanna paused for a moment.

'Well, they had enough on their plates, and I was fine, just a bit tired.'

'The doctors hadn't finished your examination. You were found unconscious on the stairs. Can you remember how you got there?' Joanna smiled as she dismissed the question.

'I wasn't unconscious; I was resting. Walking up two hundred steps takes it out of you at my age.' Rita looked at Joanna and smiled.

'Tell you what; I'll put my pen and paper away. We can start again; we were concerned for you; that's why I've come to see if you require any help. Do you need any shopping? Also, have you been able to get your pension?'

'Her hair nice. I like short hair; put clips in it with flowers.' The Chinese girl observed.

'Do you always keep your hair short? It suits you?' Joanna asked. Rita looked at her with a realisation that she would be here sometime. Going at Joanna's pace would be the only way.

'Okay, if I look at your kitchen, see if you need anything?' Walking back into the room, concerned, she said.

'Your fridge and cupboards are empty. When was the last time you ate?'

'I don't have a great appetite. I'm fine.' Joanna dismissed the question.

'I'll go to the local supermarket. I won't be long.' Joanna passed her an envelope, the address was in Chinese, but the postcode was local.

'Would you do me a favour and post this to save me climbing those stairs.'

An hour later, Rita carried two bags of shopping into the kitchen.

'I've bought you enough to last a few days. I'll put the kettle on and make you a sandwich. You must try and eat and drink; that's why you.' Pausing so as not to offend her. 'Had to rest on the stairs.'

They sat for a few moments in silence. Joanna finished the sandwich, warming her hands on the hot teacup. Looking around, Rita did a mental inspection of the flat. The sideboard drew her attention as it looked out of place with the rest of the room, as did the French and Chinese books.

'You have a large collection of foreign books.'
'I love reading them. Keeps the words in my head.' Joanna smiled.
'You can speak Chinese.'
'Yes, and I'm fluent in French.' Pointing, she said, 'I designed the sideboard myself. For me, learning a language was sitting at a piano and playing without lessons. When I speak Chinese, you hear Mai's voice. I would repeat each phrase like her. She would giggle a lot when I got it wrong.'
'Were you married.' Joanna seemed to think for a moment before she answered.
'Well, I suppose I had a husband of sorts.' The girl on the sideboard drew her knees up under her chin and said.
'I don't like him first time and last time he bad.' Joanna tilted her head as if she was listening to something.
'Mai never liked him.'
'Who is Mai?'
'That's her in that picture. I did her hair and makeup; that was the day we had a big adventure at a posh hotel. We did laugh. She wouldn't keep still. It was the first time she ever had makeup on. She was my best friend.' Mai sat up and giggled.
'Lipstick tastes funny.' Rita was becoming more curious about Joanna's past.
'Did you do languages at university?'
Joanna laughed.
'No, I'm self-taught. Well, I did have a lot of help. It took three months to get to Shanghai. That's when I met Monique; she taught me French on the way. There wasn't much else to do on the ship even though it was my honeymoon.'
'Why Shanghai?'

The Boating Lake, Toxteth, Sunday morning, Liverpool 1936.
Carrying a bible, Joanna walked in through the gates. White clouds slowly moved, occasionally revealing a crystal blue sky. People smiled and nodded their heads as they passed by. Joanna sang the last hymn of the mass under her breath. The sound of

children made her feel happy; standing still for a moment with her eyes closed, she lifted her face to feel the sun's warmth.

'I'm sorry to bother you. Would you hold my coat?' He was tall, distinguished in his forties, and dressed in an army officer uniform. Joanna jumped as he surprised her.

'Yes, what's happened.'

'I've got to effect a rescue in the lake.' Pointing to a boy about ten years old. 'His boat stuck in the middle. I'm going to wade out and bring it back.' Rolling his trousers up, taking shoes and socks off, he stepped in, splashing towards the boat. Joanna sat on a bench, watching him reunite the boy with his toy. She didn't see him give him a few coins with the hallmark of a clandestine arrangement.?

'Thank you so much. I must say we were a great team.' Taking his coat back

'I didn't do anything; you did all the work. I just looked after your coat.'

'But you did it with great skill and precision; you didn't run off with it.' They both laughed. 'I hope you don't mind if I join you on your walk. It's such a lovely day.' Joanna smiled, saying.

'Yes, that would be good. We are part of a nautical rescue team.' The captain stood to attention. Turning to Joanna, he saluted, saying.

'On behalf of the British Army, I, Captain George Barlow, honour you with an Ice cream.'

Sitting on a bench shaded by tall trees, Captain Barlow and Joanna didn't speak, enjoying the ice cream; there was an awkward silence broken when he said.

'You know I've often watched you on Sunday morning. I. could set my watch by your appearance at ten past ten every time.' Joanna was surprised.

'Yes, well, I always go to nine o'clock mass then have my walk. Mum has my breakfast ready when I get home. I've never seen you before?'

'Normally, I sit on a bench on the other side behind the morning papers. Do you live far from here? Please don't tell me as that came out all wrong. I sound like some devious fellow with evil intentions. I'll arrange a firing squad to shoot me at dawn. Please accept my apologies. 'Joanna laughed and reassured him 'I'm sure that's not necessary. I live just over the road opposite the gates. Sometimes I pretend that the park is my garden and what it would be like to be wealthy. It's a silly pipe dream.' George placed his hand on her's.

'That's not a pipe dream. It's something to achieve. You never know when opportunities come along; grab them with both hands.'

Walking back to the gates, George told her all about his army career and the exotic places he'd seen.

'I hope you don't think I'm forward, but I walk in the park on Wednesdays after tea. The camp is only ten miles away, so I drive to park my car and unwind. It would be my honour to be reunited with the boating lake rescue team. ' Joanna laughed as he shook her hand.

'Let's hope it doesn't rain.'

Twenty-six Paget Close sat in a dark narrow cul-de-sac. White steps that attempted to improve tiny back-to-back houses' drabness, every weekend, people did their best to polish and clean the front door's a thankless task as soot ate away at their labours. Net curtains offered some semblance of finery inside brown flaking window frames.

'He's a captain in the army. Sidney, did you hear what she said? She's met a captain in the army.' Walking in from the backyard, Sidney asked.

'What's all the fuss about.'

'Mum, stop shouting. The neighbours will hear you.'

'That's why I'm shouting. Mrs Jackson can hear a shilling drop in Birkenhead; God, it'll make her so jealous.'

Sidney and Agnus Smith were dependable working-class people; Agnus cleaned houses for wealthy people in big mansions overlooking the park and as a dinner lady in the local school. Sidney was a shunter moving goods on the Liverpool docks. Agnus would often impress the neighbours by saying how well Joanna was doing as a shipping clerk and then describing the palatial homes she cleaned. Sidney just sat and listened.

'Please tell me you're in love.' Agnus's cheeks blushed as she swooned. Sidney pulled a chair towards her.

'Come on, Agnus, you'll have one of your funny turns. Sit down and take deep breaths.'

'Mum, I've only just met him, I'm not in love, and he is much older than me. We are just friends, that's all. He drives to the park on Wednesday so I'm meeting him for a walk, that's all.'

'Oh my God, he has a car. Sidney, did you hear that he has a car.'

'Mum, stop shouting.'

Six weeks later. Putting his knife and fork on his empty plate, he sat back, pattered his stomach and thanked her.

'Agnus, that meal was fit for a king.' George loosened his tie and finished the last of a bottle of brown ale. Agnus flicked a tea towel at Sidney.

'Did you hear that, Sidney? Someone knows how to appreciate my cooking.? Joanna, come and help me with the plate. Putt the kettle on.' Joanna had been sitting listening as George took centre stage.

He produced a silver cigarette case and offered Sidney one. Sitting quietly, they watched the smoke curl.

'I was hoping to speak to you alone. I'm not the kind of man who beats about the bush, so I'll get to the point, your daughter besots me, and if I have your permission, I'd like to take her hand in marriage.'

'I don't know what to say; it's a bit of a shock you've only just met?'

'You seemed hesitant it isn't our age difference, is it.' George speaks with urgency

'No!. . . . Err, well she is only eighteen.' He replied, unsure.

'And I'm forty-two, but I can give her the kind of life people only dream of; she'll see the world and places you just read about. George sat closer to him.

'Well, you seem a decent man, sorry. . . I'm mean officer, and there's not much around here apart from hard graft and low pay.

'Yes, I agree.'

'Agree to what.' Agnes enquires as she walks in from the kitchen

'Agnes, I've some news. Joanna is to be married to Captain Barlow.'
'I knew it when you see true love, you know it. Wait till I tell the neighbours. They'll be so jealous.' Swaying for a moment. 'Oh! I think I'll pass out with excitement.'
'Agnes, take a few deep breaths and sit down.' Sid pushed a chair towards her.
'Now we agree there is a small window of opportunity; you see, I have to sail to the Far East in two weeks, Shanghai to be precise, so we need to get a move on with the wedding plans. 'I couldn't believe my luck was falling in love as my posting has to be a married couple.' George had a smile on his face.
'That's a bit soon. Sidney was surprised at the speed of it. Agnus hits him with a towel.
'Nonsense, Sid, what's the point of delaying? I'm sure that's the right thing for both of them. Yes, Captain, I agree.'
'Agnus, if I'm going to be your son in law, call me George.' Joanna walks in from the kitchen.
'Have I missed something?'

Joanna's flat
'That was it; two weeks later, the whole street packed the church. My mother cried; dad fought with the collar of his shirt. I walked through a daydream and down the aisle to the docks and a slow boat to China.' Joanna gazed at the sideboard as she remembered. Rita had made more tea and seemed to have forgotten why she was there.
'It sounds like something out of a Mills and Boon novel. How long did it take?' Making herself comfortable by taking her coat off.
'Three months.'
'You can fly there in a day now. So, you had your honeymoon on the high seas?'
'You wouldn't call it a honeymoon; we had separate cabins. I would ready myself every night, waiting for him to knock on the door. We'd meet for breakfast and then walk around the deck. He'd promise to pay more attention to me but had a lot of paperwork to do, 'army business never stopped,' he would say.

Then one night, the knock came. I'd put more perfume on as I opened it. The young cabin boy was out of breath as he asked me to help him with George.' Rita was fascinated.

'What happened to him.'

'He was unconscious drunk laying in the corridor. Eventually, we got him to bed. After that, I didn't see him for two days; I'd stopped putting perfume on as it was unlikely he'd call? That's when I met Monique.'

Two miles out from Marseilles 1936

The Mediterranean had been calm as the ship slowly made its way to the harbour. Usually, Joanna didn't sunbathe; the only time she chanced was in the park wearing a sleeveless dress. She dabbed her neck with ice water sunburnt from walking around the deck as she sat eating her breakfast.

'I have a cream that would help.' In her early forties, she was urbane, dark hair tied back with a silk scarf and makeup perfect, expensively dressed in a long blue silk dress. Her stunning diamond neckless glinted for a moment as she took a small jar of cream out of her handbag. 'If you don't mind, I'll put some on for you to give you some relief.'

'No, I'm fine. It'll be alright.'

'From where I stand, you might need the ship's doctor.'

'Is it that bad?' As she gently rubbed the cream on, she asked Joanna.

'Are you travelling alone I've noticed you sitting on your own most days?' Joanna nervously thanked her.

'That seems much better.'

'My name is Monique Wiseman.' Introducing herself as she sat down. 'I did see you are walking with, I presume, your father.'

'Oh...no, he's, my husband.'

'I hope I don't sound like I'm prying; let's start again. I'm Monique Wiseman. I didn't catch your name.'

'Sorry... Joanna Smith... no.. I mean Joanna Barlow, haven't got used to my new name yet only got married two weeks ago.'

'So, you're on your honeymoon?' Joanna didn't answer as the waiter handed Monique a menu. 'Just coffee, please.' Monique placed the jar of cream next to Joanna's plate. 'If you need any more, I've got a good supply, although I do pay far too much for it. Gabrielle Chanel assured me that it's the best made. I hope you don't mind, but I hate sitting alone if you're not with your father, I mean your husband; we could be dinner partners.' Joanna paused for a moment, desperate for some company; she agreed. Monique said as she shook Joanna's hand.

'c'est un plaisir de diner avec vous.' Joanna had a blank look on her face.

'I don't understand?' Monique apologises as she translated.

'It's French. It means it's a pleasure to dine with you. I could teach you French if you want, we do have a lot of free time before we get to Hong Kong. I'll have you fluent by then.' For the first time in weeks, Joanna laughed.

Marseilles

Walking into the Basilique Notre Dame, they were glad to be out of the fierce midday heat. Joanna blessed herself three times in the holy water in an attempt to cool down, whispering, 'God forgive me.' As they took in the grandeur and silence, hundreds of candles flickered, offering a feeling of peace and solemnity. Monique sat in one of the pews and closed her eyes for a few moments. Joanna made her way to the altar and knelt and prayed. Walking back up the aisle, she thought Monique was asleep. Quietly she lit candles and said another prayer.

'Do you think God answers prayers?' Joanna was startled as Monique spoke.

'Yes, I think he does.'

'Does he only pick the best ones?' Joanna didn't understand what she meant. 'Forgive me; I shouldn't have spoken that way. I lost Phillip in the last war. We were only married for two months. I prayed every day, asking God to keep him safe. You remind me of myself. I would give anything to have him back. You have George, and yet he is not with you?' Joanna replied defensively.

'He has lots of paperwork to do.'

'The other night, I took a lot of money off him playing poker. I live in Monti Carlo the cassino is my main hobby. He was writing i.o.u to the other gamblers as I left the table. Don't worry; I've settled them. I did it for you, not him.'

'I don't know what to say. George and I have never spoken about money. Monique realised she'd embarrassed her as her dislike of George had got the better of her.

'I think George had forgotten his wallet, and he'd had a lot to drink. I'm sure he'll settle his debts.' Joanna said defensively.

They didn't speak as they walked back into town. Joanna wanted to say something; instead, she slipped her arm around Monique's, linking her.

'My family are Jewish so you can imagine my introduction to God. Phillip was catholic; my father never spoke to me again. I left Paris and went to live with his brother Isaac in Vienna. They had also fallen out with each other many years before. My father was a well-respected rabbi. The split in our family was tragic. My brothers and sisters ignored me; my mother just wept. Uncle Isaac was a businessman. The only God he followed was diamonds and gold. At first, I just kept his books and looked after customers with drinks; this proved to be an unforeseen bonus.'

'What do you mean.'

'While they waited to see Uncle Isaac, they thought I was some lowly servant, so speaking openly revealing how to squeeze Uncle and how much they wouldn't pay. Some planned to get credit. I became his eyes and ears. Eventually, He gave me a greater role; it was easy as a woman, convincing a prince or king of his Mistress's best piece. One morning I arrived at the office to find him dead at his desk; he'd had a heart attack, as he had no children; you can imagine my surprise when they read his will. He'd left everything to me. We have Jewellery shops all over Europe. When we get to Hong Kong, I'll be staying there for a few weeks. We must keep in touch as your French is coming along; you're a good student.'

'I'll write to you every day.' Joanna said excitedly.

'Yes, you will, but only in French that way, you'll keep the words in your head.' Monique pointed to a small café and sat down in the shade, speaking to Joanna, she said.

'a le serveur pour le menu.'
'Can we have a menu, please?' Joanna asked the waiter.
Monique laughed, correcting her.
'No in French.'

Bombay
The routine was the same day after day. George would appear at midday to apologize to Joanna walk around the deck a few times convincing her he'd give her his full and undivided attention when they get to Shanghai, then disappear back to his cabin. Joanna stood at the ship's front as they approached Bombay, gazing at hundreds of small boats. Monique asked her to come ashore as soon as they docked.
'I've never seen a hotel so big.' Joanna kept looking up at the ceiling.
'I'm meeting a diplomat who's acting on behalf of a Raja. We have a new collection, so I'd like you to put some of the necklaces on be my model for the day.' Joanna's head spun as each piece dazzled the diplomat; also, she'd drank a glass of champagne for the first time. Hiccups and a fit of giggles added some entertainment to the presentation. Walking back to the ship, Monique couldn't stop laughing.
'He was paying more attention to you than the jewellery.' Joanna, still fighting the hiccups, replied.
'He had a wedding ring on; he should be ashamed.' Monique smiled as she said.
'tu as beaucoup a' apprendre.'
'I've learned so much these last few weeks.' Joanna qualified the statement in English.
'You're getting there.' Monique smiled.
Walking up the gangplank, George was waiting for them holding out his hand, steadying them as they stepped onto the deck.
'I bet you two have been on an adventure.' George sounded suspicious. Joanna lied when she said.
'No, we just went for a walk to look at some gift shops.' Monique thanked Joanna and made her way to her cabin. George's face darkened as he questioned her.
'Has that French woman said anything to you.'

'No, what do you mean.' She saw a side of George she hadn't seen before for the first time.

'Did she say anything about last night in the saloon?' George bit his lip as he waited for her reply.

'No, she talked about her family in Paris and losing her husband in the war.' George's face softened.

'Well, that's good to know. Let's walk for a while; sadly, I've just received more paperwork; the British army never sleeps.' Joanna's flat.

'You didn't tell him about the hotel and trying on the jewellery.' Rita asked.

'No, I felt like a naughty schoolgirl. He didn't like Monique. My French was now perfect. Monique gave me some books in classic novels; I absorbed myself in the characters; one story described people making love naked. I didn't know that was allowed. It was a shock for me, although I did go back and read those pages a few times.' Both of them laughed.

'It's so commonplace these days that's all you see sex on the TV.' Joanna thought for a moment.

'I haven't got a TV, Mabey. I should get one.'

Rita looked at her watch, then jumped up.

'Joanna, I'm sorry I didn't know the time. I'll call back first thing in the morning.' Mai sat up on the sideboard and spoke.

'I like her; she has a nice face with no lies.'

'You know Mai would say you have a nice face with no lies.' Rita was confused.

'I don't understand.'

'Mai would say if you have a sour face, you can see dragon scars. When you tell lies, an evil dragon cuts your face leaves his mark.'

'Well, Mai is right. I promise you I'll only tell you the truth.'

Singapore

At breakfast, Monique sat quietly, listening as Joanna described how much she liked the character in one of the books as exciting and funny.

'il est intelligent, exciant et drole.' Monique didn't answer. 'Is everything alright?' Joanna asked.

'Things are not good in Germany when I try to keep in touch with my relations; some of them have stopped writing to me. It's very worrying.'
Walking through the streets of Singapore, young children came up to them with small trinkets. Joanna wanted to buy everything. Monique had to stop her. Eventually, they arrived at a beautiful hotel; its shaded garden welcomed relief from the humidity.
'What is it called.' Joanna gazed at the cocktail.
'It's a Singapore Sling.'
'I'm not sure I don't want the hiccups.'
'Just have one.' Monique laughed as she encouraged her.
After two drinks, Joanna didn't have the hiccups, but she did have a smile on her face that seemed to be stuck. Making their way back to the ship, children approached them, selling trinkets. Joanna playfully began to skip and turn circles; the children followed her, laughing; they copied her as they went.
'Be careful; you'll fall over.' Monique cautioned her, laughing, Joanna replied.
'You sound like my mother.' She stopped, put her head down, and burst out crying as she said this. At that moment, homesickness overwhelmed her. Monique hugged her; Joanna held her tight as she sobbed.
'c'est bon de pleurer .' Monique sympathises with her.
'I don't know what's wrong; it just hit me; I missed them so much.'
'Tell me about your parents.'
Linking her arm, Joanna told everything about her family, how her mum is in competition with one of her neighbours, and how her dad always wakes her up with a cup of tea before he goes to work. A cooked breakfast would be set as she returned from church every Sunday. They spotted George on the far side of the road in an alleyway arguing with a man as they approached the harbour. Walking across the street, Joanna kept looking back at him. Monique felt her unease.
'We'll have tea and cake when we get back; I'll teach you how to play backgammon.' Joanna didn't answer.
The banging on her door dragged her from a fitful sleep.

'Joanna, are you alright.' Monique asked. Opening the door, Joanna stood for a moment, confused. 'When you never came for an evening meal, I assumed you were tired when you missed breakfast. I thought it best to call on you.'

'What time is it.' Trying to tide herself up, she realised she'd slept all night in her clothes.

'Well, they have set the places for lunch. Shall I order you something, or would you like a Singapore Sling you could sleep until Shanghai.' Laughing, she replied.

'No, I'll stick to water.'

Joanna's flat.

'Where was George?' Rita engrossed in the story asked. Mai answered.

'He should fall in sea big shark eat him.'

'He came back that night. Monique said he was in the saloon; for a few moments, I imagined he'd fallen overboard.'

'If he had, what would you have done?'

'I'd have got off the ship in Hong Kong with Monique, but then I'd have never found Mai.' Joanna looked at the sideboard.

'There is something I need to ask you. Would you consider living in a residential home? You'd have your room, and there are no stairs to climb.' Joanna thought for a moment. Mai spoke.

'Who would move sideboard, my brother, in Shanghai with the cart.'

'If Mai was here, she could ask her brother to move the sideboard on his cart, but he's in Shanghai.' Joanna gazed at the sideboard. Rita sighed as she answered. 'Well, think about it. I'll make another cup of tea.'

Hong Kong

'We dock at six o'clock in the morning; I'm hoping to go ashore at eight-thirty.' Joanna didn't answer as they sat eating breakfast in silence. Picking her bag up, Monique rummaged in it and then handed Joanna a small box. 'This is a keepsake for you. If we hadn't met on this journey, I would have jumped overboard at Gibraltar.' Joanna eye's full of tears opened them and gazed at a cameo with a bird swooping its wings open. 'It's a white kingfisher my uncle gave it as a birthday present. When I think of you, I'll see you wearing it and remember all the adventures we've had.' Joanna knocked a cup of tea over as she hugged Monique.

'I don't know what I'll do with you.' Joanna whispered.

'You'll be strong and find your way. Love will come; give it time.'

'George is a stranger to me. I don't know why I'm here.'

'When you settle in Shanghai, things will get better; look at how you learnt a new language; did you ever think you could.'

'No.' Joanna sobbed

'Well then, have confidence, trust your feeling. I need your address in Shanghai?' Joanna had memorised it some many times, wondering what it looked like.

'Fleur House, Nanking Boulevard.' Monique wrote it in a small notebook then gave her a business card. They walked in silence on the quey side for a while; then, the call came to board the ship. Monique hugged her one last time then spoke in French.

'j'aime plus ma douce amie, Au revoir'.

Joanna's flat

'That's so sad. It must have been awful for you.' Rita listened in the kitchen as she made lunch.

'When I got back to my cabin, there was a parcel outside my door. Monique had left all her books, enough to keep me entertained until we got to Shanghai.'

'Did you see more of George?' Rita had taken her shoes off and made herself more comfortable.

'Yes, I did; we had breakfast a few times, although he read the paper while we ate. He did introduce me to some of his drinking friends, business people and a few diplomats; the way they looked at me made me shiver. I couldn't wait to get to Shanghai; I'd had enough of the ship. It felt like a prison, and I missed Monique so much.' Mai speaks.

'Madam Chung, make us clean house over and over until fingers bleed. She says important people come to whip us if house not shine.' Joanna paused for a moment.

'Mai said they were exhausted cleaning the house, waiting for our arrival. That's when I met her for the first time, and it didn't go well. I couldn't remember when I spoke to someone young

Mai was my age. I did laugh a lot with Monique, but everyone on the ship was years older than me. I needed people my age.'
Mai laughs as she speaks.

'Madam Chung says take bags to the bedroom. I ran towards her, but she thought I stole the bag.'

Shanghai Fleur House

The weather was warm and sunny as the ship made its approach. Joanna could see Shanghai in the distance. The smell of perfume and sweet fruit overwhelmed her as the wind gently enveloped her. The buildings reminded her of the Liverpool waterfront. In the harbour, hundreds of small boats with all kinds of goods swelled the tiny decks, flowers, fruit, pottery, and women washing clothes and hanging them on lines that ran the length of their floating homes. She caught sight of a woman soaking two small children in a tin bath, the children flicking water over the side, laughing. The quayside was a hive of activity, packing cases inside nets lifted onto cargo ships. Horses were pulling more goods on wagons waiting patiently in long lines. The clatter and bangs from ships being repaired close by competed with people calling out and the occasional ship's horn echoing around the bay. Joanna closed her eyes and absorbed all the sounds and smells.

'Penny, for your thoughts?' George crept up beside her; before she could answer, he continued pointing to an extensive black limousine on the quayside. 'That's our ride to your new home. They'll bring the rest of the luggage later.' George sat in the front, talking to the driver in army uniform. Joanna is on the back seat with a small bag and Monique's books. Driving along, she marvelled at the scene crowds of people, some carrying bales of cloth on their heads. One man had a long pole over his shoulder with pots and pans swinging from it as he walked quickly, lines of horses pulling more cargo to the docks, and small barefoot children running alongside. On the corners of the streets, Vendors cooked food from makeshift kitchens. Everywhere she looked, rickshaws carrying people about in chaotic race, missing each other by inches. Taking in the grandeur of the tall buildings, for a moment, you thought you were in London. The road then became less busy driving along a wide boulevard; she gazed up at beautiful mature trees in blossom. On either side of the road, the houses were as big as a palace. Black iron railings protected extensive front gardens,

some with willow trees moving gently on the wind. The first time she saw the house, it took her breath away. It looked like the French chateaux on the cover of one of Monique's books, tall and elegant, large windows with storm shutters folded back. A terrace wrapped its self around the upper floors. The entrance had two large polished wooden doors; she could see her reflection in them. A poorly dressed Chinese girl picked her bag up. Joanna grabbed the handle and pulled it back.
'Let go.' Joanna shouted.
'No, I take.' Mai begs her as they struggle.
'Indeed, you want, I'll call the police.'
The front door opened; an older Chinese woman dressed in black stern-looking grey hair tied back walked out, raising a stick to hit her. Mai sank to her knees, crying.
'I try to take bag to bedroom.'
'You know this person.' Joanna stood in front of Mai as she asked the woman.
'Yes, I do; she's not very good. Please accept my apologies. I'm Madam Chung's housekeeper; this guttersnipe will be punished.' Kicking Mai, she swore at her in Chinese. Joanna handed the bag to Mai and then spoke.
'It's just a misunderstanding; please show me the way to my bedroom.' George walked up the steps laughing.
'Are you causing trouble, darling? You've only just arrived?' Madam Chung curtsied as she spoke to him.
'It's a great honour to have such a distinguished guest in the house; please let me show you to your room.' Ignoring Joanna and Mai, they walked into the house. The staircase was sweeping, and carved bannisters led up to a landing with stairs on either side leading onto a gallery that squared off the upper floors. Madam Chung guided George to the right.
'This is the master bedroom; your balcony looks out onto the gardens.'
As Joanna and Mai got to the top of the stairs, Mai pointed left.
'Your room is this way, mistress.' Joanna looked at George as he disappeared into his room. She had thought about what would happen when they arrived at the house, would she start waiting for the knock on her door or would they share a room,

the arrangement looked like separate rooms after three months of sleeping on her own then nothing had changed but would he knock on the door? Her bedroom was as big as her house back in Liverpool. Large windows open to a balcony that looked down to a vast walled garden with a pond traversed by a wooden footbridge. A king-sized bed covered with white sheets against the wall opposite the windows. Two tall black, lacquered wardrobes with flower patterns embossed in the doors stood on either side of the bed. Joanna stood in disbelief at the richness of the room.

'I sorry, mistress, you can beat me now.' Mai was kneeling on the floor, her head bowed.

'Why would I do that?' Joanna shocked.

'I disrespect you.?

'No, you didn't; it was a mix-up. Please stand up; what's your name.'

'Mai Chow, please beat me, Madam Chung, happy if you beat me. Make her smile.'

'I'm not going to beat you. How old are you?

'Eighteen mistresses.'

'You're the same age as me. Tell me what do you do here.' Joanna smiled at her.

'I'm a snivelling little dog who good for nothing that name of the job.'

'That's awful; why would they say that?'

'Also, gutter rat and from murdering river people.'

'Stop! please stop.' Joanna sits on the bed 'dear God, this is terrible. Let's talk about nice things. Ask me a question.'

'I get in trouble told not talk to mistress.'

'That's not going to happen; ask me a question; please stand up, sit next to me.'

'Where you come from? You very beautiful, your dress pretty, what colour is your hair? Will you have babies? Are you a princess? What do you like to eat? Everyone in the kitchen talks all time before you come. Do you have your maid.?' Joanna studied her face, gentle and smooth, her eyes dark as her short hair and an infectious smile. She was the first Chinese person she had ever had a conversation with.

'Slow down all in good time but first, where did you learn to speak English?'

'For three years, I work for the British diplomat. I learn words.'

'You're excellent.'

'His wife, strange lady.' Mai whispers.

'Why? Joanna whispers back.

'She spends a lot of time in the back of a car with chauffer she says they are looking for earing; windows steamed up I think they make a pot of tea.'

'You're so funny.' Both of them giggle

Joanna's flat.

'From the moment I met Madam Chung, I was afraid that she governed with a wooden stick. Always polite with me, but a hint of disdain in her comments. She knew her place with George fawning and praising him whenever they spoke. I didn't see Mai for weeks, well, I did see her but only from the window when she was working in the garden. She waved at me one morning. I had to watch Madam Chung beat her for doing so.

'That's awful. Did you tell George what did he say?' The social work sounded angry.

'He'd say it's the way they do things here; then he'd take himself off to his bedroom.'

'You still had separate rooms.'

'After the first week, George started going away for a few days. I began exploring the house; it had a small banqueting room used as a ballroom with a grand piano, glass mirrors polished every day. I'm sure Madam Chung had secret passages throughout the house as she would just appear at any moment. I ate alone most days, even when George sat with me, hiding behind a newspaper. I longed to go out and explore, then one morning Madam Chung informed me I had visitors.'

Shanghai

Descending the stairs, she could hear voices from the drawing-room. Three women in their forties stood admiring a painting over the fireplace. Well-dressed with wide brim hats, all three had matching pearls and parasols.

'Ah! You must be Joanna. I'm Agnus Mason-Taylor. Major Taylors wife. Can I introduce you to Cathryn Frobisher, Colonel Frobisher's wife and Marjory Cummings, the ambassador's wife? I hope you've settled in.' All three of them looked her up and down one of them whispered.

'She's so young.' Before Joanna could answer, Madam Chung, pushed a trolley in with cakes and tea.

'How thoughtful; let's sit down and get to know you. First, you need to know a few things: we have a very vibrant woman's club, organising bridge and whist clubs and afternoon tea dances. It's Colonel Taylor's birthday ball; next week, we are in the arrangements' final throws. I'll make sure you have your invitation before then. Is your husband available?' It seemed Mrs Agnus Mason -Taylor did all the talking as the other two just frowned at Joanna. Before Joanna could answer, Madam Chung spoke.

'I'm sorry, the master is away on army business.' The three women looked disgusted at a household staff member interrupting their conversation. Joanna could see their dislike.

'George will be back tonight. I'll make sure I tell him.' Cathryn Frobisher enquired.

'Can you tell us a bit about your background?' Joanna answered nervously

'Well, . . I come from Liverpool. I live with my mother and father.'

'And what line of business are they in?' Mrs Frobisher asked, eager to know.

'Well, my father works on the docks shunting cargo, and my mother cleans houses.' The three of them looked at each other with a scowl on their faces; moving close, they began a whispered conversation, the occasional word could be heard 'yes I agree with import and export and pioneer in the modern woman. Mrs Mason -Taylor spoke.

'We have a monthly newsletter and a section for newcomers. Your father's thriving import and export business contributes to the economic wealth of the Empire. Your mother is a pioneer in the entrepreneurial spirit of the British woman with her domestic service company. Are we all agreed with that?' The rest of them nodded their heads. 'I will add that the Chinese business community widely reads the newsletter and, in turn, provides us with many opportunities.' Mrs Frobisher was next to ask Joanna.

'Have you decided on your ball gown? We must know what colour you've picked.'

'I'm afraid I haven't got one.' Mrs Mason -Taylor rummaged in her bag and handed Joanna a business card.

'The address is on the Bund; Raymond Pasquale runs designs Creatifs he'll look after you. Hopefully, he doesn't speak in French to you; he seems to think everyone can speak that dreadful language.'

'That won't be a problem. I speak fluent French.' All three women look at her as if she had just confessed to a murder.

The following day Joanna picked the phone up and dialled the number on the card.

'bonjour puis-je parler a M. pasquil.' They spoke for a few moments and made an appointment later that afternoon. As Joanna looked for Madam Chung, she noticed the car waiting outside.

Joanna jumped as Madam Chung appeared behind her at the top of the stairs.

'He'll wait for you and bring you back.'

The shop was on the Bund, and as she stepped out of the car, all the wonderful chaos that she saw the first day driving to her new home was still franticly running about in all its glory. Raymond Pasquale was a small, thin man with slick backed hair and a pencil moustache. He was dressed immaculately in a pinstriped suit. Joanna remembered one of Monique's books he must have modelled for the role.

'Madame per ici s'il vous plait.' Taking her hand, he guided her inside. They spoke in French for about five minutes, after which he complimented her. Speaking in English, he said.

'You must have had a good teacher. I assume you'll need a ball gown for the Colonel party. I would normally recommend many designs, but I struggle to have them ready on time. I have a collection of what you British say is 'off the peg'. You have a lovely figure. I'm afraid a figure like yours will cause a lot of jealousy; that's the price of beauty.' Joanna blushed, not too used to compliments. 'There is one dress that I would like you to consider.' He disappeared into the rear of his shop; looking out the window, she longed to walk as far as she could taste freedom again; she felt like a prisoner in the house. He guided her to a changing room. Inside, the dress was hanging up; it was simple cream silk with lace piping around the collar with a hint of gold in the stitching. Trying it on, she stepped outside.

'merveilleux superbe. You'll break many hearts; that's another price of beauty.'

'I'm sure my husband might have something to say about that.'

'Forgive me; I thought you were single. Do I know your husband? I've often attended many functions at the embassy.'

'His names Captain George Barlow but we have only just arrived from England.' His face darkened his friendly smile disappeared.

'I'll wrap the dress up for you.' After she changed, he opened the door, holding her hand; he sounded concerned.

'You must take care of yourself. Promise me you'll be careful, don't be frightened to stand up for yourself.'

Joanna was surprised at how he changed when she mentioned George's name. What did he mean when he said to be careful? Arriving back at the house, George met her on the steps, and he didn't look happy.

'Madam Chung said you went shopping. Did you speak to anyone?' Joanna was shocked why he was so angry.

'I went to get a dress for the ball. The only person I spoke to was the owner.'

'Well then, that's good. I was worried about you. There are many thieves and robbers in Shanghai. I wouldn't like something to happen to you. If anyone talks to you, you must let me know.'

'Why?' George hesitated then answered.

'It's . . .because. . I do sensitive army work. I must admit apologies; I might have overreacted.'

Later, Joanna sat looking at the dress laid out on the bed and confused at what Pasqual said and George being so angry. She wished Monique was here; she would know what to do.
Joanna's Flat.

'I didn't understand why George was so angry with me. The next few days back in my prison watching Madam Chung abuse the kitchen staff. Shanghai was an enormous city, the buildings on the Bund were amazing, but it was a tiny place to me. I hadn't seen anything; those buildings were like distant mountains. The house was huge, yet the walls were closing in on me. I couldn't breathe. I was bored then I found a magazine with an advert *'Why don't you design furniture yourself we make for you.'* So that's what I did; sitting down with a pen and paper, it seemed to draw its self. I rang them and made an appointment. That's it over there; on the front of it is a kingfisher I copied it from the broch Monique gave me.' Mai speaks.

'Kingfisher, show us the way he protects us.' Joanna smiled then said.

'Mai would always say kingfisher will keep us safe. While we ate breakfast, I asked him If he would escort me to the furniture factory behind the newspaper, saying he was busy but asking Madam Chung. I suppose that's his way of apologising. That's when Mai came back into my life.'

Shanghai
The knock on her door woke her up; she thought George was ready for her; in a panic, she wasn't prepared for him. Then she realised it was morning, the sun bursting through the window. Another knock then the sound of Madam Chung's harsh voice.

'Mistress, can I come in.' Relieved it wasn't George, Joanna replied.

'Yes, please come in.' As Madam Chung slid inside, Mai followed her and stood with her head bowed.

'Master George has informed me that you have an appointment at a furniture factory. This person will go with you. She will speak Chinese if you need interpretation. You must report to me if she has bad behaviour and might steal; boat people are thieving scum.' As Madam Chung left them, Mai knelt on the floor.

'Mai, what are you doing.' Joanna was surprised at her kneeling.

'I pay you respect. Madam Chung says I must kneel before you and only walk in your shadow.'

'Mai, stand up and promise me you'll never kneel again. I want to show you something I've designed my sideboard.' As Joanna opened the drawing Mai gasped.

'Mistress, it's White Kingfisher; how do you know White Kingfisher? He precious to the Chinese people.'

'Monique gave me a pendant with a Kingfisher on it; I just copied it. Why is he so important?' Joanna pointed to her bed, where they sat. Mai looked around in case Madam Chung was listening, whispering she told the story of the Kingfisher.

'The moon deity was a fierce Warlord. He lived in a palace on the moon. Every night the moon would be complete and shine so bright that people could see like daytime, but all people have to praise him every night and leave gifts. One day The Moon deity come to earth and fight a great war. The Moon deity killed Prince Choe.

When his sister Michan finds out, her heart becomes dark with sorrow and cries for a hundred days. When she stopped crying, she refused to praise the Moon deity. He became furious and made his way to Michan's palace.

She asked the gods to help her. The gods took pity on her and granted her wish. She wanted him to feel grief and pain. She wanted him to touch her sadness. The Gods tell her that only white Kingfisher can help, but he has to drink her tears, but she has none left. That night she has a dream and her brother Choe's spirit; he sings a song they sang as children one tear fall from her eye. White kingfisher flies through the window and drinks a tear. Michan waits in her garden for the Moon Deity. For one moment, the White Kingfisher touches the ground where beautiful flowers grow to show the way to peace, love and happiness. Moon Deity sees her and raises his sword, but Michan asks him, before you kill me, I ask one favour: you smell one of the flowers, he does, and his heart melts like butter in the sun. He feels her pain and sorrow. Ashamed breaks his sword and goes back to the moon, where he tries to hide the moon; no matter how hard he tries, people can still see the moon; when it is full in the sky, candles are lit in memory of Michan.

'Mai, that's a beautiful story.'
'Mistress, I tell you something, but I get in big trouble if they know I tell you.' Mai looked around as if she was about to be caught telling a lie.
'Tell me what?'
'Madam Chung, say Mr George want to know if men talk to you.'
'What men?'
'Just men.'
'I don't understand? Tell me exactly what did they say?'
'If men talk to you, I have to tell them. Madam Chung says she beat me if I don't tell them.' Joanna stood and walked around the room for a few moments. Putting her hat and coat on, she turned to Mai and spoke.
'Well, then we'll have to talk to as many men as we can. If they don't know, then they won't find out.'
'Mistress, I can't tell a lie.' Joanna smiled and then whispered.
'I'm not asking you to lie; just don't tell the truth.' Both of them laughed as they left.
Mai sat in front of the car as they drove to the factory. The road took them through the British sector; it was as if they were going through one of the hundreds of prosperous areas of England, with elegant mock Tudor frontages, and expansive gardens with manicured lawns. Road names in English. Mason Road, Prince Albert Avenue, Victoria Mews. Two well-dressed gentlemen, with silver, topped walking sticks, strode purposely along at the corner of one road. Joanna asked the driver to stop. Rolling the window down, she asked.
'I'm sorry to bother you, but is there a post-box nearby.' The two men took their hats off as one of them, a young man in his twenties, spoke with a soft Scottish accent.
'Two roads from here; you can't miss it.' As he leaned on the window, she touched his hand.
'Thank you so much. Isn't a lovely day.' The young man smiled as he winked at her.
'It is now.'
'Thank you. Goodbye.'

Mai and the driver looked at Joanna through the rear mirror, shocked. Mai spoke to the driver in Chinese. The driver looked frightened, then shook his head as if to say 'no' to something. The factory was a two-story building with long windows; the entrance looked like the front of a hotel. It even had a concierge dressed in a top hat and tails holding an umbrella. The manager met her on the steps; he spoke excellent English. As Joanna walked up the steps, Mai followed her with her head bowed. Guiding her to his office that looked like the shipping office in Liverpool, it even had a large framed photograph of George V1. After looking at Joanna's drawing, he smiled.

'You have an eye for design; I'll make sure we will have our best people working on it. It will be ready in one week. Can I interest you in a tour of the factory?' As she inspected the work benchers, the carpenters bowed as she went past. Outside he politely helped her into the car, holding her arm. Driving back to the house, Joanna looked in the mirror; she could see a smile on Mai's face. Madam Chung met them on the steps of the house.

'I trust you were able to find the factory.' Her face said more, and her attempt at a smile failed. 'Mr George is waiting for you.'

George was sitting at the dining table with a large brandy in his hand.

'Ah! There you are, please sit down. I need to make you aware of something. It seems that tensions are growing between the Chinese and the Japanese. It happened before back in thirty-two. It's nothing to worry about, but you need to be careful to try and avoid the newspapers. I'll be going away for a few days so that Madam Chung will see your needs. I'll be back in time for the ball.' Joanna had a feeling of dread in her stomach. The prospect of being alone in her prison frightened her.

'I want a maid of my own.' George laughed as he answered.

'You don't need a made Madam Chung will see to your every need.'

'I want a maid to help brush my hair and sort my clothes.' George sighed as he gave in.

'Very well, you can have a maid.' George finished his drink

'I want Mai; she speaks English.' Joanna felt confident and determined. Madam Chung didn't give George time to answer.

27

'That is a big mistake she will steal off you, also. Are you prepared to beat her? If Mr George says it's alright, then she will be your maid.' George didn't answer; he looked at his watch and left the house. Staring at each other for a few moments, Madam Chung spoke.
'Will that be all.'
'No, send Mai to my room. I need her to brush my hair.'
Later that afternoon, Joanna sat at her dressing table; Mai gently brushed her hair, looking at each other in the mirror. Joanna had a smile on her face; Mai couldn't stop giggling. Joanna turned to Mai and whispered. 'She wants me to beat you, so I need you to cry out in pain. We'll pretend you didn't do it properly.' Shouting 'You! Stupid girl. 'Joanna clapped her hands. Mai cried out as they stifled a laugh. Somewhere in the house, Madam Chung smiled.

Joanna's flat Tuesday at 9 am.
Walking unsteadily up the hall, she opened the door. Rita was carrying bags of shopping that she placed in the kitchen and making breakfast. Joanna called out.
    'I'm not very hungry; you don't have to go to any trouble.' Rita replied.
    'I'm making a full English for both of us, and also, I picked up your prescription. Doctor Kinsella said that you hadn't had one for six weeks. I promised him you start taking his medication; we don't want you resting on the stairs again, do we.' Carrying two plates, she handed Joanna her meal. 'It's my day off today, and as my husband is decorating the lounge, I decided to escape; you don't mind, do you.'
    'No, I look forward to your visits.' Joanna smiled. Mai speaks.
    'We never see the doctor my mother make potions; she makes tonic from fish brains.'
    'Mai told me that they were too poor to see a doctor; her mother made all kinds of remedies. You don't pay a doctor when you are sick; you pay him to keep you healthy; I suppose when you get ill, you can always blame him.'

'The last time I was here, you were telling me about a ball you were going to.'

'Oh! Yes, that ball.'

Shanghai

Joanna walked up and down the bedroom in her ball gown; turning gracefully, she acknowledged an imaginary person with a wave of her hand. Mai sat on the bed, laughing as she spun around, holding the skirt out.

'What do you think? Do you like the colour?'

'Mistress, you look like a wealthy lady who is a princess.'

Both of them froze as Madam Chung knocked on the door.

'There's a phone call for you.' Joanna followed her down the stairs; the phone was on a hall table.

'Hello.'

'Mrs Mason -Taylor here. I'm checking in with the details for the ball. I've put you and George on table nine with a few people from the chamber of commerce. What colour dress did you pick?' Joanna noticed the draw on the table was open. Inside were lots of envelopes with George's name on them. She looked at some of the different addresses: The Carlton Hotel, The British International Hotel, Singletons Night Club. The postmarks were nineteen thirty-three and thirty-four. Her head began to spin; she always thought this was his first time in Shanghai. 'Hello, are you still there? What colour dress are you wearing?'

'Oh! It's cream in colour.' She started trembling.

'That's good. I'm in pink, although I'm not sure it makes me look like a pot of jam, be there eight sharp must go.' Joanna took a few letters out and ran back up the stairs. Sitting on the bed, she opened them. They were all bills asking for immediate payment; one said they could no longer extend his credit. Looking at Mai, she asked her how long she had known George.

'First time I see him at ambassadors house at a party.'

'What year was that?'

'Four years ago. Mistress, why you look unhappy.'

'I'm confused. I thought this was George's first time in Shanghai?' Changing the subject, Mai said.

'Mistress, I tell my mother men and woman dance very close, my mother says that sinful. Will you and Mr George dance.'

'I've never danced with George. Mai, let's do something happy I need cheering up.' Walking over to her dressing table, she put the letters away.

'I show you the Chinese celebration dance.' Mai stood in the middle of the room and began slow movements with her hands, pointing her feet and turning; the movements became more intricate as she twisted, making circles. 'Mistress, I learn your dance; just follow me.' Joanna copied Mai falling over a few times, then she improved, over and over, the movements were soft and graceful; Mai started singing in Chinese as the dance progressed. Joanna concentrated hard as she matched her every move. When they finished, Joanna, out of breath, said.

'Mai, that was wonderful. I feel amazing.'

'That's why it called celebration dance to make everyone happy. Mistress, will you teach me your dance.' Joanna thought for a moment, then started singing.

'Keep young and beautiful; it's your duty to be beautiful; keep young, beautiful if you want to be loved.' Skipping sideways, she did a soft shoe shuffle and repeated the dance. Mai clapped as Joanna stopped pointing the finger at her emphasising the verse. *'Take care of all those charms, and you'll always be in someone's arms, keep young and beautiful if you want to be loved.'* Mai joined in clumsy; she soon got the hang of it, even the little tap dance Joanna did at each turn. Taking hold of Mai's hand, she spun her around without thinking pulled her close. The kiss happened a deep passionate kiss. Mai's arms fell to her sides as the embrace overwhelmed her. Shocked, Joanna pulled away in horror.

'Mai. . . forgive me. . . I don't . . .Oh! God. . .I don't. . .please forgive me.' Mai is standing. Still, the eye's closed, her lips pouting spoke.

'My first kiss, I melt like butter in the sun.' They looked at each other for a few moments. The windows were open, in the distance, the sounds of the city. Birds were busily singing as they went about their business in the garden. Slowly Mai walked over to Joanna, slid her hands around her waist and returned the kiss,

Joanna attempted to pull away, but Mai pulled her closer. The moment seemed to last forever as they melted together. Sitting on the bed holding hands, they didn't speak, unsure what to do next; Mai broke the silence.

'Mistress, is this what love feel like? I love my mother and father and all my brothers and sisters; this is not the same. I want to laugh and cry?' Joanna had tears in her eyes as she whispered.

'Yes.'

'Mistress, I have to go. I have work to do. Madam Chung beat me if I don't go,' Stopping at the door, smiling, she turned and spoke.

'Leave the window open.'

The light faded, casting long shadows as the wind teased the curtains. Still wearing the ball gown, she could still feel Mai's kiss lying on the bed. Deep inside, she felt joy and fear, excitement and doubt, then longing to see Mai again, craving to kiss her. The room was now dark, but the moon made a welcome appearance bathing the room in soft light. The clock on the dresser said midnight. She hung the dress up, made herself ready for bed. She didn't hear Mai climb through the window. They looked at each other for a brief moment. Joanna made the first move as she slowly undressed Mai, who helped Joanna out of her dressing gown. Standing naked, they kissed. Laying on the bed, they looked at each other for a while then their lives changed forever. Each touch, each caress, took them on a new journey. In that moment world outside no longer existed; a new excitement full of possibilities and joy now belonged to them. Holding Mai's hand up, she gently stroked each finger.

'Mai, tell me about growing up on a boat; what was your childhood like.' Mai thought for a moment.

'Every day was full of noise and play. Some night when it is hot, I sleep under the stars, and when you hear people making babies, babies cry all night, but they keep making babies. All boats are very close; Mr Lau live on his own he snores like he is cutting wood for a new boat. My brothers get no sleep, so they cut his rope and push him out into the river one night. He has gone for days. People say he went to America looking for a new wife.'

'What happened to him?' Mai laughed as she told her.

'He comes back with new swear words for my brothers. They laugh and drop their pants to show him their bottom.' Both of them stifled the screams of laughter. Slowly sleep crept on them as the two lovers floated away.

The following day the knock on the door sounded like an explosion. Mai had gone, then she heard George's voice, in a panic, she dressed.

'Are you decent? I need to speak to you?' Opening the door, he was standing there with a piece of paper in his hand. 'you're good a French, could you tell me what this say's?' Joanna quickly read it out loud.

'Il ya quatre choses que chaque personne a plus qu'ils savent, les péchés, les années de dettes et les ennemis.'

'Yes, that's good, but what does it mean in English.' He was impatient for an answer.' Joanna translated.

'There are four things every person has more than they know, sins, debt, years and foes. There's a small drawing of a green snake on the bottom. Where did you get it?'

'It was delivered to the Officer's Club; good well done, it's the ball tonight, so be ready at seven.' George walked away briskly.

Joanna's flat.

'I'd never known joy like it; every fibre of my being seemed to come alive. It was so liberating I felt I could fly out the window across the city and the mountains beyond. We were so innocent we knew nothing of physical love, and yet everything seemed so simple, so perfect. Georges knock on the door brought me back down to earth.' Rita had a tear in her eye as she asked.

'Where was Mai? How did you keep it a secret?'

'She came to my room, she kept her head down, but I could see her smile, then she started giggling. I tried to ask her to help me get ready, but we couldn't stop laughing. As she brushed my hair, she bent down and kissed my neck. We looked at each other in the mirror, not saying a word, just looking at each other. Mai knelt on the floor as I put makeup on; when I finished, I made

her sit and put makeup on her. That's when I had my brilliant idea.
'What was that.' Rita hadn't stopped smiling, listening to her story.
'We'll I told Mai that I would dress her in my clothes one day, do her makeup and hair and we'd sneak out the house and have tea in one of the hotels on the Bund.'
'Wasn't that dangerous?'
'Oh! Yes, but exciting, we held each other then I left. Sitting in the back on my own, George sat in the front, talking to the driver. As we drove up Nanking Road, a group of people stood in the middle, looking at something on the floor. Two men had been shot. The car stopped for a moment; a British soldier came over and spoke to George; he said someone had assassinated two Japanese businesspeople. I did hear him say, let's hope it doesn't kick off; those bloody Chinese students have formed a little army.'
'Why did they do that.'
'You have to understand that China and Japan had been fighting for years. Japan had invaded China years before and fought many skirmishes until it settled down, tensions had been growing for some time, and there were many stories of killings in Shanghai. They set up protection zones for foreigners. If it did start, the zones would be a place of safety.'

Shanghai, The Ball.
George opened the car door and held his arm out for Joanna to link him. There were two giant porcelain dragons on either side of the hotel doors; the entrance hall was illuminated by a massive chandelier with a wide curved staircase leading up to a ballroom with eight smaller chandeliers. A jazz band played ragtime, and a few couples were already dancing inside. George seemed to know everyone by name as he said hello. At their table, George introduced Joanna. Looking around, the wives of the businessmen were a lot older than her. A waiter brought a tray of champagne and handed everyone a glass. She was just about to drink when one of the women informed her that it was for the Colonel's toast. She wanted to run out and find Mai; then, she

heard men arguing behind her. They were speaking in French about the assassination. One said he blamed the British for constantly negotiating behind their backs; another said the students' behaviour was costing him money. Then she heard a familiar voice; it was Mrs Mason -Taylor.

'Ah! There you are, here's your raffle ticket. Are you free Tuesday afternoon? We're having a tea dance at the Hilton that starts at two? Have you noticed anything.? Joanna looked around but couldn't see anything. 'I'm in blue; that pink disaster made me look like a bowl of Eaton mess must go.' Joanna watched her go from table to table like a bee in high summer. Behind her, she heard one of the men swear; even in French, it's 'fucking British.' The room went dark, the band started playing happy birthday, and the colonel walked in. His speech was about grit, resilience, commerce and endeavour. George didn't speak; he kept looking at his watch. Halfway through George left, the night's entertainment a display of Scottish highland dancing saying he had to talk to someone. Joanna was relieved as she didn't fancy dancing with him. When the dancers finished, guests were directed to the terrace at the rear of the hotel to witness a firework display in the Colonel's honour.

As they made their way, she noticed George being poked in the chest by a man in military uniform, the way George was holding his arms out; he looked like he was apologising for something. Finding a quiet corner, she wondered how much longer the evening's torment would take place, desperate to go home and see Mai.

'So, you're the pot.' He was tall in his thirties, holding a bottle of champagne; swaying slightly, he spilt some of it on the floor. Joanna moved away from him, saying.

'Excuse me, do I know you.'

'Find a room for the night you could get to know me better. I bet you taste sweet.' George appeared and grabbed him by his arm.

'Alister dear boy, there you are, come and have a brandy with the Colonel,'

'I wouldn't piss on him if he were on fire; it's a waste of piss; I'm fine here, just me and the pot.' George had to drag the man away. Joanna made her way back to the table. Picking up her scarf and handbag, she had to get out as soon as possible; she felt the walls closing in on her, panic set in, she was about to run out when a voice called.

'Ah! There you are, number 86, that's you.' Mrs Mason - Taylor handed her a small plant in a blue pot. 'You just missed out on the vintage wine, never mind. Why are you leaving so early?'

'I've got a bit of a headache.'

'It wasn't the Colonel's speech, was it? I did tell him to say a few jokes.' George attempted to interrupt them. Mrs Mason Taylor didn't look at him as she said. 'I hope you're feeling better; goodnight.'

'I'm sorry about Alister; he can't hold his drink.'

'He kept saying I was the pot? What did he mean?' Glaring at him for an answer.

'I haven't the foggiest darling. Are you alright?' Joanna didn't answer; she gave him the plant pot. 'Give this to Alister. I think he's been looking for it.

'I must make apologies; I'll see you to the car. Sorry, darling, I have to stay a bit longer on army business.'

On the way home, she wanted the driver to go faster; the window was open, and a cool breeze came in; closing her eyes, she felt calmer. The image of the dead bodies road and the drunken man terrified her; she just wanted to hold Mai. Madam Chung met her on the steps.

'I trust your night went well.' Joanna held her emotions in; she didn't want to burst out crying in front of her.

'Can you send Mai to my room first thing in the morning? I need her to help sort out my wardrobe.' Without changing, she lay on her bed and cried herself to sleep.

The following day Joanna sat on her bed with Mai next to her. She relived the events of the night before, occasionally wiping her eyes and blowing her nose. Taking a deep breath, she told Mia she had a brilliant idea.

'No! No, Mistress, that would be dangerous. Madam Chung would beat me for a long time.'

'How would she know. I've picked out your outfit with shoes to match; your feet are the same size as mine, I can do your makeup. We'll dine at the Hilton, have afternoon tea. They'll think you're a wealthy lady well connected. Men will tip their hats at us.' Mai had a shocked look on her face.

'If someone talks to us, what name do I have? If they ask who my family what do I say.'

'If they do, just say shipping.'

'What name of the ship.'

'It doesn't matter; they won't ask. I've even picked a name for you. She was a character in one of the French books, Chen Zhao.' Mai shook her head.

'No Mistress, what if Chen Zhao is in Hilton Hotel? She is very angry.' Joanna laughed, saying.

'I'm afraid she's unavailable as she jumped off the Eiffel Tower in chapter six.'

'Mistress, I scared. when we do this.'

'That's the hard bit avoiding Madam Chung; we don't want her to see you all dressed up.' Mai thought for a moment then said.

'Every few weeks she has a day off, she doesn't leave the house, her brother shit face Fu Chung visit, they drink all day, she falls a lot then sleep all the next day.'

'Why do you call him shit face?'

'He in charge of all sewers in Shanghai; that why we call him shit face.'

The knock on the door made them jump; it was Madam Chung. Joanna grabbed a handful of clothes from the wardrobe and threw them on the bed; opening the door; she called back to Mai.

'You stupid girl, how long is this going to take.'

'I sorry, mistress.' Mai replied, smiling as she started folding the clothes with her back turned.

'You have a delivery of furniture a cabinet; do you want them to bring it up. While I'm here, I could beat gutter snipe for you.' Her sickly grin turned Joanna's stomach.

'I'm quite capable of doing it myself.'

They sat looking at the sideboard. Joanna had placed different items on it, ornaments, pictures, and jewellery, not satisfied she re-arranged them. Then she changed them again; eventually, she settled on the first choice.

'Mistress, can I ask you something.' Joanna leaned close to her.

'Oh! I hope it's gossip or a dark secret.'

'Why do English people say sorry all-time.' Joanna gave her a quizzical look.

'What do you mean?'

'Well, they say 'sorry is this chair taken', 'sorry have you seen my umbrella, they say sorry can I have a spoon.' Joanna gazed into her face, slowly pulling her closer and kissing her.

'Mai, I'm sorry, but I love you.'

The knock on the door made them jump; it was Madam Chung. Joanna opened it to gaze at her suspicious scowl.

'There is a phone call for you.'

'Hello.' It was Mrs Mason Taylor

'Ah, your there, Agnus Mason Taylor here. Are you decent for the lady's guild meeting Wednesday at two pm? It's at the Richmond Club, not my choice; service isn't up to scratch, they haven't got a clue how to make a decent cocktail, well must go! See you Wednesday.' Joanna stood with the phone to her ear for a few moments, wondering what to do; as the line was dead, she couldn't answer. Wednesday morning Mai helped her get ready.

'Come with me.' Joanna said excitedly

'No! No! not possible.'

'Well, travel with me, at least you could do that, or maybe you could wait outside.' Mai thought for a moment then said.

'I wait here for you if I go; I look like a sore with a big thumb.' Joanna smiled, saying.

'Spoils sport, I'll just have an adventure on my own.'

A military car pulled up next to her as she walked to the tram stop. The driver was a private.

'Captain Barlow arranged for me to take you to the Richmond Club.' Joanna thought for a moment; she didn't tell George she was going; how did he know. 'He said I should wait and bring you back.' She listened to him sing; he had a good voice. 'When I get back to Blighty, I'm signing up with a travelling show you might see me on the west end Tommy Crowther England's finest crooner, once I get an agent, the sky's the limit.' The Richmond Club overlooked a small park with a bandstand at its centre. Waiters in white coats busily served drinks. The club had seen better days threadbare in places; the large French windows gave it an open feel. Mrs Mason Taylor appeared.

'So, you made it, I was wondering if you'd come; we're in the Topaz room. I didn't make the arrangements, not my choice; the curtains don't match the carpet, but what do you expect? it looks like a French boudoir, whatever that means.'

'It's a woman's bedroom.'

'Oh! Dear, you speak French, well, never mind.'

The room was full six-woman to each table, a long desk in front of a small stage with Cathryn Frobisher and Marjory Cummings pouring over paperwork.

'I've placed you on the newcomer's table; the minutes of the last meeting are available; I'll leave you to it.' Mrs Mason Taylor sat at the head of the desk, pushing the other two to one side, her status being the guild chairwoman had to be maintained. Joanna was the only person on the newcomer's table who drew the gaze of the rest of the audience. She heard the occasional whispered comment, 'so that's her' and 'she's so young.' The meeting moved quickly; a dispute developed between the knitting club and the Wednesday book club. Someone had changed their venue to clash simultaneously; the debate went backwards and forwards like a Wimbledon tennis final. Joanna did her best not to laugh as one of the knitting club members full of passion remarked that the knitting clubs were of national importance.

'Your better suited to have warm feet in a trench rather than a book; knitting clubs saved the feet of thousands of soldiers in the great war.' The knitting club won the day, humiliated the book club rearranged to Tuesday mornings nine-thirty. They broke for lunch after arguments about seating arrangements for the Polo tournament. Marjory Cummings, the ambassador's wife, sat next to her.

'I hope you don't mind me asking. Do you have any friends of your age?'

'Well, yes, I do have a friend; she's older than me.' Joanna couldn't say Mai was her best friend. 'Her name is Monique Wiseman; she's in Austria runs her own diamond company.'

'You should have friends your age. I've heard that name before; I worked in Paris before I met the ambassador.' Holding her hand up, she pointed to a ring. 'I'm sure he bought this off her. My mother was French, so it's my second language; all the ladies in the guild think speaking French is a cardinal sin.' Joanna whispered.

'je peux parler francais.'

'Thank God, I'd like to invite you to my house for tea if that's alright with you. Promise me we'll have conversations in French. I get very little chance to speak it.' She sounded like Monique, passing her a card. 'here's my phone number. I hope you call me; sitting in a roomful of dinosaurs will drive you mad.' As she left the table, she held her hand tight for a moment as if to reassure her. After lunch, the mood changed; an army captain addressed the meeting on the agenda; its title was 'Safety on the Bund.' He terrified the audience with tails of murder, abducting, and kidnappings without mincing his words. He reminded all the ladies to carry an umbrella and a whistle and then show them how to poke an assailant's eye out.

'Why can't we be allowed to carry a pistol.' Cathryn Frobisher asked as a gasp rippled like a small wave around the hall. His reply was mocking.

'We wouldn't want to make matters worse; by the time you'd rummaged around in your handbag, you'd be dead, or the assailant had fled; in your case, a whistle and a stout umbrella alerting people for help would be enough. Always travel in pairs and keep your umbrella close.' Nervous at first, Joanna enjoyed the proceedings; she couldn't wait to get home and tell Mai how ridiculous the meeting was. Private Crowther, the England's finest crooner, leaned against the car smoking as Joanna approached.

'All done for the day, are we.' Opening the door, he asked, 'Is there anywhere you'd like to go? The car doesn't have to be back until five.' Joanna smiling, replied.

'No, I need to go home, thank you.' She could see herself sitting on her bed with Mai falling about laughing. Running up the stairs, she called to Mai, but there was no answer. Looking out the window, Madam Chung was sitting on a bench drinking with 'shit face'. Eventually, she found the gardener in a small hut tucked away at the side of the house, full of tools; he lay on a small bed in the corner, photographs of his family on the wall next to him. Jumping up, he bowed his head in Chinese; he apologised if the Mistress was looking for him; he must have done something wrong.

'I'm looking for Mai.' He was relieved that he wouldn't receive a beating; he informed her Mai's mother was about to give birth Mai had to go home. This news hit her like a thunderbolt. Running back out of the house, she would go to the Bund and find her, but how? There are hundreds of boats on the river.

'Forgot something.' The singing private was sitting in the back of the car, smoking in no hurry to get back to the camp.

'I need to go to the Bund.'

'Bilymey love, don't you read the papers? It's too dangerous.' Joanna turned on her heels and walked away.

'I'll get the tram.' Starting the engine, he followed her.

'Alright, I'll take you but sit in the front. There's a pistol in the glove compartment. I have to keep the bullets separate; God knows why I'd be full of bullet holes; that's stupid army regulations for you. What's the panic?'

'I have to help a friend.'

On the corner of the tram stop, white-shirted students had gathered. A blood-soaked man lay on the ground; local police tried to form a circle around him, but they could not stop the odd kick. The private commented.

'The students have formed a protest army; anything that's sniffs of Japanese gets a kicking.' One of the policemen stopped them, asking where we were going. Joanna answered in Chinese.

'We are going to deliver a baby.' Smiling, he waved them on.

'Good God, you speak their lingo, aren't you clever. I hardly say the Kings propper like.' Joanna wasn't sure if he was joking.

'This friend of yours, does she have an address.'

'No, all I know is she lives on a boat; her Name is Mai Chow.'
'Bloody hell, there are hundreds of boats. Start asking questions they don't take kindly to white people.'
'Just drop me off. I'll be fine.'
As they drove along the bund, there seemed to be more boats than ever. Ahead of them were roadblocks. Pulling into a side road, the private turned the engine off.
'Listen, miss; I'll get court marshalled for this. I'll wait here for as long as I can; I'll say the car broke down. Come back in one piece.' Walking along the road towards the roadblock, a soldier approached her. She convinced him she was a nurse on an emergency call. Surprised, he said he'd accompanied her, saying.
'They're all scum on these boats.' Out of earshot of his comrades, he changed. 'My family came from these people; my uncle still lives here. I have to pretend I hate them.' Relieved, Joanna asked hopefully.
'I'm looking for a Mai Chow her mother is having a baby. Your uncle knows them.' Turning right to their left at the end of a long wooden boardwalk; the river flowed fast, no longer visible from the road; they stopped at a small boat with a hand-built cabin. Placing his rifle on the deck, he called out. A frail older man opened a window. For a few moments, they embraced, then the older man remonstrated with the soldier for putting himself in danger. Joanna spoke in Chinese.
'I'm looking for Mai Chow her mother is having a baby.' Smiling, he pointed to the other side of the river.
'When they make noise, no one sleep, so the boat stays there until the baby is born.' Looking across, she could see a longboat with a large cabin at one end and what looked like a canvas tent at the front.
'I need to go over there. Can you help me?' The two men looked at each other. The soldier disappeared for a moment; his uncle offered Joanna a drink of apple juice. He warned her not to cause his nephew any trouble as she sat drinking. Two-man appeared in a small rowing boat; one of them kept pulling the oars against the river's flow. The soldier further along the

41

boardwalk knelt and pulled up a rope that went across to the other side.

'The rope helps them to get across. I have to go; you can find me at the checkpoint.' Helping her into the boat and began rowing as the other man pulled on the rope, keeping a straight course. Slowly inching their way, she could see lamps inside the tent casting shadows against the canvas. A young man appeared and stood at the back of the boat, pulling the rope tight as the smaller boat pulled alongside. Joanna spoke in Chinese.

'I need to see Mai.' The young man gazed at her for a few moments, then held his hand out and helped her on board; he disappeared into the tent. She noticed a tarpaulin sheet draped over some boxes; the wind lifted it briefly to reveal four children sleeping; after a few moments, Mai came out with a look of horror on her face.

'No, no, you must go; you can't be here this bad, very bad.'

'Mai, I had to see you.'

'Madam Chung will beat me; Mr George will be very angry.'

'She's drinking with shit face; George is away. Has your mother had the baby?' Mai shook her head.

'Baby won't come out three days; she tries, but she very weak. She might die.'

'Can I help? I want to help.'

'Do you know how to bring baby,'

'No, I don't; what can we do? Can't she go to the hospital?'

'Hospitals want money; they won't treat people like us.'

Mai's mother moaned inside the tent as Mai's father wiped her face with a wet cloth. An older woman fanned her all the time, rocking backwards and forward, praying. Joanna and Mai knelt beside her and took over. Mai's father lit a cigarette as he left. Mai's mother opened her eyes and smiled at them for a moment.

Joanna's flat

'We did our best, but she was getting weaker, then it dawned on me there might be someone who could help.' Rita engrossed in the story asked.

'She wouldn't go to the hospital; what could you do?'

'Marjory Cumming the Ambassadors wife, I had her card in my purse; it was her only chance. I told Mai I would get help. As we rode back, I prayed and prayed she would help us. The soldier sat by his uncle's boat eating out of a bowl; he was surprised when I asked him to escort me to a phone box. At the checkpoint, a captain started screaming at the soldier. I yelled back in Chinese and demanded to speak to his superiors; this worked as he panicked and agreed. That's when I met the White Russian.'

'That's a cocktail, isn't it?'

'No Shanghai became a home for Russians escaping the Bolsheviks; many of them were from the educated class, teachers' dancer's musicians deemed enemies of the revolution. The prosperous ones built a new life in China; the rest lived off the land; the only problem was they had no nationality; they called them The People from Nowhere. When she answered the phone, I went blank for a moment; then everything came out so fast she couldn't make sense of what I was saying. Take deep breaths; she kept saying. There was a long pause then she told me to stay by the phone. It seemed ages, of waiting; I felt sorry for that poor soldier nervously watching his superior. I was about to give up when the phone rang. She told me to stay, and a doctor would meet me. His name was Dimitri Volkov his arrival wasn't inconspicuous as I watched a white Rolls Royce complete with a chauffeur stop in front of the checkpoint. He was a small man rotund with a ruddy complexion and sandy hair. He was impeccably dressed in a pinstriped suit. He was one of the attending surgeons to Tsar Nicholes and his family. He delivered some of their babies.'

Shanghai the checkpoint
The chauffeur took two leather bags out of the car as another argument with the captain started. For a few moments, pointing a gun at them, he demanded to know what was going on. Speaking in English, the doctor shook the captain's free hand.

'Please to meet you. I have a patient who needs my attention.' Confused looking at the bags, he asked about their contents. He told them to continue after gazing at the surgical instruments, but the chauffeur had to stay. The soldier was now carrying the two bags and his rifle. The captain told him to report anything suspicious, although this meant he had more time with his uncle. As they walked, Joanna said.

'I can't thank you enough for helping us.' Pausing for a moment, he explained to her.

'I am in debt to Marjory Cumming; what I do tonight is only a small token of appreciation.' Looking at the boat, he said, 'Oh! This is exciting. I must warn you I can't swim.' He winked at Joanna as he stepped into it. The crossing was more straightforward as the river was moving slowly now the rains upriver had stopped. Before they landed, he'd taken his coat off and rolled his sleeves up. Mai's brother took the bags and followed him into the tent.

'How long has she been in labour.? He asked as he felt her belly; Mai replied.

'Three days but baby won't come.'

'The baby is the wrong way round. I'll have to turn it.' Taking a small jar out of his bag, he poured olive oil over her swollen belly and then pushed and massaged it. Mai's mother cried out for a moment as Mai cradled her. Joanna took her mother's hand and held it tight; even though she was exhausted, she had a firm grip. After a few moments, he stopped, satisfied; he took a set of forceps out of his bag.

'I need you to lift her head; ask her can she feel the contractions.' The answer was yes. 'She needs to push.' Joanna could see the baby's head as he inserted the forceps; slowly, the baby came out, placing the little girl on her mother's chest; he removed the afterbirth. Mai spoke.

'You must give that to my grandmother.' Curious, he asked. 'Why?'

'She will offer it to the river spirit as thanks.' Joanna couldn't speak as tears filled her eyes. The doctor called for Mai's father.

'How many children have you had.' Mai translated.

'Ten.' The doctor shook his head as he said.

'Number eleven will kill her, do you understand, no more babies.' Mai's father nodded his head in agreement then shook his hand. Drawing the canvas back to leave, the rest of Mai's family stood in front of them, smiling and bowing, the little ones touching Joanna's dress as they went. Mai threw her arms around Joanna, squeezing her so tight they nearly fell into the river.

'I'll come to the house tomorrow night.' With a knowing smile, she looked into her eyes, saying, 'leave the window open.' Mai then hugged the doctor; taken aback at first, he grabbed her hands to instruct her.

'You look after your mother; she must rest.' Making the return journey, he remarked. 'I delivered one of the Tsar's babies, in a room full of amber, on a table that belongs to Napoleon, and now a baby in the poorest of settings in a makeshift tent on a boat, the struggle is the same bringing new life into the world.' The soldier was sitting with his uncle eating out of a bowl as they approached; quickly picking his rifle up, they made their way back. Joanna glanced back across the river, Mai waving back to her. The captain seemed to lose interest in them as he waved them away through the checkpoint. The doctor offered her a lift; Joanna pointed to Tommy Crowther fast asleep in his car.

'It's been an adventure this evening; you and your friend did an excellent job assisting me. I wish I could have our little medical team celebrate tonight's success, but sadly I leave Shanghai next week for the United States of America.' He said this loud with a sense of pride. 'If I could give you some advice, leave Shanghai as soon as you can. I see all the same signs I saw in Russia. Shanghai has been my home for so long, but it breaks my heart to see it falling apart.' Taking her hand, he kissed it and then left. With his mouth wide open, Tommy, snoring, woke with a start as she tapped on the window.

'Shit, look at the time I'm done for, they'll shoot me.' Quickly turning the engine on, he drove off and then broke hard to let Joanna in the front. She reassured him.

'When we get back to the house, I'll telephone your commanding officer and recommend you receive a commendation for keeping me safe. I'm in a happy mood to sing one of your songs.' Relaxed, he sang.

'Happy days are here again
The skies above are clearer again
Happy days are here again.'

True to her word, she called his camp and spoke in glowing terms about how helpful he'd been to her, apologising for his late return. Tommy stood in the doorway and gave her a thumb's up as he left. The house was quiet, with no sign of Madam Chung exhausted; she climbed the stairs. Without undressing, she fell into a deep sleep. The following day Madam Chung woke her; you have a phone call; it's Marjory Cummings. As she watched an unsteady Madam Chung struggle down the stairs, she hoped she'd stay in bed for the rest of the day, sleeping off the hangover.

'Dimitri told me she had a baby girl.'

'Yes, the baby and Mai's mother are ok. Thank God he came. I don't know how to thank you enough.'

'Well, you can thank me by coming to lunch at my house. I'll send my driver to pick you up. It'll be 'le the de l'apres-midi,' just the two of us and

Would you please talk in French? It's so dull the ambassador is away at the moment I need cheering up.'

She watched a long black limo sedan with a small British flag at the front parked outside. Joanna hoped it was the 'singing private Tommy Crowther'; sadly, he was older, bald with a face that said, don't talk to me. Dressed in a black suit with a prominent stomach that struggled to stay behind his belt, pointing to the empty seat in the back, he grunted as Joanna said hello. She was about to start a conversation with him, but the glass panel behind him made it pointless. Driving along tree-lined avenues, she imagined what it would be like to be a princess waving to adoring crowds. The car turned into a long-manicured driveway with willow trees on either side; it was a mansion house with a fountain outside. Six Roman columns supported a huge terracotta roof. The entrance was under a stained-glass canopy as a butler opened the door and welcomed her.

'Please follow me.' He guides her through a stately entrance hall; for a moment, she thought she was in an art gallery—tall porcelain flower pots standing on Italian marble tiles with garlands of flowers hanging down. A painting of the king looking down guarding the occupants. 'The ambassador's wife is in the summer house; it's the other side of the lake.' Walking onto a terrace overlooking a lake with a single swan gracefully gliding along. She could see Marjory sitting in front of a small glasshouse next to a table. It reminded her of the palm house in her park in Liverpool. As Joanna approached, Marjory called to her.

'Would you like a drink.' She lifted a large jug. 'I have Singapour Sling, or I could make you a cocktail.'

'Just lemonade is fine.'

'Now sit next to me and tell me about this new baby.' Joanna was surprised at how drunk she was as it had only turned midday.

'I don't have much experience of babies; seeing one born was incredible; she had a fine head of black hair. I couldn't believe it.' Marjory was excited listening to her.

'Oh! I wish I could have been there; you're so lucky. Dimitri gave me a running commentary. He said his journey across a raging torrent full of sharks.' Joanna was confused. 'He made it sound like an expedition; he does exaggerate a bit that's Dimitri, then he was accosted at the point of a rifle, he said it was better than being chased by the Bolsheviks; through the streets of Moscow.'

'Was he chased?' Joanna wanted to know more about him.

'Yes, he was; he took a bullet in his shoulder before escaping, unbelievably he removed it himself.'

'I'd like to meet him again.' Joanna asked.

'I'm afraid that might not be possible he leaves in two days.' She looked sad as she gulped her drink down.

'He told me he was going in two weeks; he even showed me his American passport. He said you helped him.' Pulling her close, Marjory looked around as not to be heard.

'Can you keep a secret? You see, I've done something very naughty; I need you to promise me you'll keep a secret. Dimitri tried to get a British passport, but the ambassador wouldn't help. I had a contact at the American embassy who said he would. He needed a letter of endorsement supporting his application. Are you sure you won't have a drink?' She attempted to fill a glass.

'Are you alright?' Joanna was shocked the confident woman who sat next to her at the woman's guild was desperately unhappy

'No, I'm not; I hope he doesn't find out what I've done.'

'What have you done.' Pausing before she answered, she whispered.

'I forged his form, copied the ambassadors signature. The contact called me to say they were checking all the paperwork, and they'll want additional information; they're sending out a new form. If they contact the ambassador, then I'm in deep trouble.'

'Can't you explain you were trying to help a friend?'

'My relationship was more than a friend; we'd been seeing each other for some time. Maurice found out and forbid me to see him. Dimitri has the passport, and If he leaves before they ask for more information, he'll be in America, and it'll be too late to stop him. I can't stand living here a moment longer, but where could I go.'

'But this house is beautiful.' Joanna felt she had to change the subject.

'It's a mausoleum, a prison. I hate it.'

The butler approached them, asking.

'Will madam be taking lunch.' With a drunken smile and a few hic-ups, she replied.

'Just a few sand wedges and another bottle of gin.' As he walked away, Marjory remarked. He's his eyes and ears reporting back when I fart.' The two of them started laughing. 'You know he has his dirty little secrets. I could make it very difficult for him, but who would listen to a woman?' Joanna became worried for her.

'They say a secret told is no longer a secret.' Marjory went quiet for a moment then said.

'I hardly know you, but I believe I can trust you; I have no one else to talk to, he thinks the sun shines out of Hitler's arse. That man will sort Europe out; he would say, his little lapdogs of diplomats agree with him. They meet here pretending to hold a Cricket Club meeting, but all they do is drink, smoke cigars and fawn over what the Nazis will do. I've even heard them say they blame the Jews for the unrest.'

'I don't understand he's the British Ambassador; how can they say such things.'

'That's not all he received a letter from the Duke of Windsor. I watched him read it and then throw it in the fire. God knows what was in it, but the rest of the day, he had a smile on his face. That night he convened an emergency meeting of the Cricket Club; by the sound of their excitement, someone must have scored a hundred.' Joanna was shocked.

'This is awful.' Marjory gave a sarcastic laugh saying.

'It is a man's world they can do what they want. I fell in love and will be disgraced. I don't feel too good; help me to the house.' Walking back, a swan followed them for a while; holding Joanna's arm, she remarked. 'I've given the swan a name Churchill. He waits for me every morning; like me, he has lost his true love, one of the Ambassadors friends who were drunk shot the pen. I can still hear them laughing; poor Churchill is waiting for an answer and a reason why.'

One of the maids attempted to help Marjory up the stairs; she waved her away. The bedroom was huge, with a marble fireplace. Everywhere she looked, there were glass and porcelain ornaments; the walls were tastefully decorated in blue, with large open windows with lace curtains that fluttered as the wind blew through. Joanna helped her onto the bed. Shaking her head from side to side, Major lamented.

'What am I going to do? Dimitri will be arrested; I don't care about me; he doesn't deserve it.' Joanna covered her with a blanket and watched her fall asleep.

Joanna looked back at the mansion; in the middle of all the grandeur was a broken heart, and she felt so sorry for her. Mai was waiting at the door when she arrived.

'Mistress, you look sad.'

Later that evening, they lay next together. Joanna told her everything.

'I'm afraid both of them have no way out; it's awful.' Mai sat up.

'My cousin work in the post office. He carries special bags.' Joanna was confused.

'What special bags?'

'When I work for the diplomat, he gets a special bag with letters.'

'Diplomatic mail.'

'Yes, my cousin, get lady's letter before husband.'

'Mai, this could be dangerous. Your cousin could get in trouble.' Mai shook her head.

'Mail always goes to the wrong house, the diplomat on phone shout a lot, happens many times no one finds out. Lady fixes paperwork my cousin put it back in the office.'

Marjory sat in the palm house, looking at her hands as the plan sank in.

'What if it doesn't work? Everyone will be in trouble. Dimitri will be arrested.'

'Mai said they complain all the time about mail going missing. If this works, your husband will never know. Once I have the envelope, I'll bring it to you.'

Joanna's Flat

'What would have happened if you were caught?' Rita had a hundred questions. 'Was the ambassador a German spy? Did the plan work.' Joanna laughed.

'You sound like a reporter. Yes, we got away with it. Mai met her cousin and gave me the letter. Marjory's driver picked me up, and we had tea in the palm house; the questions asked for information on financial transactions. Marjory forged it, and I took it back.'

'Tell me she left him and followed Dimitri.' Joanna's face saddened.

'I saw her many times after our big secret; we'd look at each other with a knowing smile. Sadly, there was no happy ending; they moved to Singapore when the war started. Then Japan invaded; her husband was lucky he was in India, Marjory was taken prisoner, she survived the war, but her health wasn't good; she passed away in nineteen fifty.'

'That's so sad.' Rita complained. Joanna changed the story.

'Not long after Dimitri's escape Mai and I had our big day out.'

Shanghai
Shit Face sat in the garden as Madam Chung carried a bottle of rice wine and two glasses. Joanna and Mai watched them from the bedroom.
  'How many bottles did they drink.' Joanna looked at Mai for an answer.
  'Last time eight, she sleeps for two days.'
Later in the day, they sat at either end of the bath; Joanna made bubbles with her hands. Mai made gentle waves with hers. Mai asked her a question.
  'Mistress, tell me the story of your God again.'
  'Well, there's the father, the son and the holy ghost.' Mai interrupted.
  'The ghost is the little bird, but they don't keep it in a cage; they all live in one body, they must be pleased sharing one body. Is the bird a chicken?' Joanna tried not to laugh.
  'Yes, they're happy sharing a body, but the ghost isn't a bird; he's a spirit.' Mai was still confused.
  'You say he a bird, now he, not a bird?'
  'Well, in all the pictures I've seen, he appears as a bird bringing light and a message from God. We call it the holy trinity.'
  'Is the light a lamp like the other story you tell me of the Genie? If the bird finds a lamp, the Genie can tell the two gods where to find the gold, gods like gold.' Joanna splashed Mai as they both laughed.
The following day there was no sign of Madam Chung as they listened for the sound of someone taking a beating; all they could hear was the birds in the garden. Joanna looked at Mai in a yellow summer dress and matching hat. She was unrecognisable; she looked beautiful—Joanna in pink with a decorative umbrella and white hat.
  'Mai, you look gorgeous.' Mai did a twirl, saying.
  'My family in the boat with lots of money.'

'No, Mai, you can't say that; they are in shipping; whoever asks will assume you're rich.'
They walked unnoticed out the back of the garden through a door into a busy road. A tram stop took you into the city on the far side. Linking arms, they giggled as they crossed; a businessman lifted his hat as they approached. Whispering, Joanna said.
'Just smile at him.'
The sense of freedom almost overwhelmed them as the tram turned a corner towards the stop. Mai had a panic attack. Pulling Joanna close, she said.
'Mistress, I can't breathe. I'm frightened.' Joanna spoke softly to her.
'I won't let anything happen to you—your safe with me.' The tram doors opened; the businessman took his hat off and gestured with his hands for them to go first. Thankfully the tram was empty, slowly making its way towards the city and the Bund; this gave both of them time to gather themselves. Like two children going on holiday, curiosity and excitement merged into one as their smiles grew bigger. They didn't speak as they took in all the busy activity of Shanghai. Joanna had a tight hold of Mai's hand; This made her relax. Eventually, the tram stopped outside the Metropole hotel. Standing, Joanna had to pull Mai to her feet.
'Mistress, couldn't we stay on tram longer.' Mai had her head down as she spoke.
'Mai, lift your head walk with confidence, remember your family are in shipping.'
Stepping off the tram, they walked towards the hotel entrance— a concierge dressed in a long black coat with gold buttons walked towards them; Mai squeezed Joanna's arm, fearful he would chase them away. Bowing, he guided them towards the hotel entrance—the long reception desk made of dark oak in front of a glass wall with green foliage handing down gave it a mystical feel. Porters were moving swiftly with suitcases towards elevators and people of all nationalities mingling in casual conversation.
'Will you be dining today,' He was an older Chinese man who spoke excellent English; carrying a notebook, he took a pen out

of his pocket, 'My name is Mr Charlie, what name shall I tell the restaurant?'

'Mrs Joanna Barlow and my friend Chen Zhao.'

'Would you like the rooftop restaurant or a private booth in the main lounge?'

'It's rather windy today; we don't want to lose our hats; the booth will be fine,' Joanna spoke with a clipped English accent. Bowing his head, he pointed.

'Ladies, please follow me.'

'Mistress, what wrong with your voice.' Mia whispered.

'I'm talking posh.'

Following Mr Charlie, they walked towards the restaurant; everywhere they looked was rich and expensive. Beautiful women in the latest fashions, business people and military personnel are all in deep conversation. A mixture of Chinese and European art adorned the walls on walnut panelling, flower arrangements in large terracotta pots, and deep red carpets leading down a broad set of stairs into a vast restaurant with private booths on each side. Waiters with short white jackets busily deliver meals to tables. In the booth, the seats were blue leather. On either side were curtains for extra privacy. Mr Charlie spoke.

'Before you look at the menu, we have seabass and suckling pig as a special today; the chef will cook it to your liking. I'll send the wine waiter over.' Clicking his fingers, he calls the waiter.

'Two Singapore slings, please.' Joanna spoke like a seasoned drinker handing the wine list back.

'Mistress, this exciting they think you a queen,' Sitting quietly for a few moments and looked at all the diners. Mai kept commenting on the colour of a particular dress. They both ordered seabass followed by cream cakes.

'This drink makes me feel strange.' Mai's smile was comical.

'Have you ever had alcohol?'

'No mistress, first time like your kiss.' Falling against each other, they laughed hysterically. Other diners looked at them, smiling at the sound of their laughter. The woman stopped in front of them, and for a few seconds, Joanna wondered who the voice belonged to, Mrs Cathryn Frobisher, with a stern look on her face.

'Mrs Barlow, are you celebrating something?' Joanna froze, unable to speak. Mai, giggling, said.

'My family in shipping.' Joanna woke up saying.

'Yes, this is Chen Zhao. It's her birthday today.' With disdain written on her face, she replayed.

'Congratulations, we were wondering why you didn't attend Mrs Mason -Taylor tea dance the other day.' Joanna wanted to ask her why she didn't use their Christian names, always formal and loud. To make things worse, she developed hic-ups. Mai didn't help the situation when she said again.

'My family in shipping.'

'Well then, I'll leave you to your festivity. The women's guild is meeting on Friday; I'm sure you'll find a window of opportunity in your busy diary, goodbye.' Her parting comment was dripping with sarcasm. Joanna watched her walk to the other side of the restaurant and sit with a group of women.

'Mai, we need to go.' Before they could move, a man with a camera appeared.

'Would you like your photograph courtesy of the hotel? It's free.' Looking into the lens, he stopped 'those smiles won't do, sit closer and cheese. I just need your address; you'll get it in a few days.'

Making their way out of the hotel, Mr Charlie approached them. In a panic, Joanna told Mai.

'We haven't paid the bill; what are we going to do? I haven't got any money, only enough for the tram.' Mr Charlie smiling, asked.

'I trust the meal was to your liking.' Joanna had to come clean and tell him she couldn't pay; she'd get George to send it to them.

'I'm sorry, but regarding the bill.' Mr Charlie stopped her.

'It's nice to have a generous admirer; It's all paid for.' Joanna broke out in a sweat as she looked around.

'Who was it.'

'Well, he asked me to be discreet. I can't tell you.'

Walking quickly across the road, they got on a tram. Joanna felt someone was following them. Her mind was racing as she wondered if George's drunk friend was there. She hadn't noticed Mai had fallen asleep. Groggily Mai held onto Joanna as they opened the garden door. She looked around to see if Madam Chung was waiting with a big stick. Sitting under a blossom tree, a kitchen girl was smoking. Mai spoke.

'Mistress, we can go, Madam Chung still in bed.'
'How do you know?' Joanna whispered.
'Smoking is forbidden; she kills you if she catches you.'
They lay on the bed, exhausted.
'Mistress, this happiest day of my life.' Sitting up, Joanna said.
'I'm sorry I shouldn't have asked you to do it.'
'Do what?' Mai looked at her, confused. Joanna stood and paced up and down the bedroom.
'Put the dress on. I never want you to take it off.'
'Mistress, I have to take it off when I clean the house.'
'No, Mai, you don't understand you should dress like this all the time, be able to go wherever you please, wear makeup, be my friend and not a maid. Let's run away.' Joanna said excitedly.
'Where will we go.'
'Liverpool, we could get a house. I'll go back to the shipping office; you could sit next to me, your good at English. We can walk in the park on a Sunday, and my mother will make us breakfast.'
'Will we keep chickens.' Joanna looked at Mai as she asked this question, realising it was an impossible dream.
'I wish Monique were here; she would help us. She would know what to do.'
They hadn't noticed the phone ringing or that it had been ringing for some time. Mai opened the door and looked down the stairs.
'Mistress Madam Chung always answers; she must still be asleep, or she might be dead.' Mai smiled as she said this.
Joanna walked down the stairs; as Mai changed her clothes and picked the phone up, a man spoke.
'puis-je parler a M. Barlow s'il vous plait.' Joanna answered in English.
'I'm sorry, Mr Barlow isn't here. Can I take a message? I'm his wife.'

'Ah, you are Joanna.'

'Yes, can I ask who you are?'

'Tell your husband Mr Autile called.' There was a pause, then he said, 'I hope you enjoyed your meal.' The line went dead.

Joanna ran up the stairs and closed the door. Sitting at her dressing table, she struggled to breathe.

'Mistress, are you alright.'

'There was a man on the phone he hoped we enjoyed the meal.'

'Did he say his name?'

'Yes, he said it was Mr Autile.' As she said, Mai gave a scream that woke Madam Chung up. In a panic, Mai shut the windows and drew the curtains.

'No! No! this bad, this very bad. We go to Liverpool now hide in your park.' Joanna grabbed Mai and hugged her as she sobbed.

'Mai, tell me what's wrong.'

'Autile is the green snake; they say he killed a thousand people. He bad man he owns Shanghai runs all the brothels, and all opium has a green snake on the bag.'

'Don't be scared; the police will protect us.' Mai shook her head as she replied.

'He pays police; they do his work. If they take a prisoner to a cell, Autile waits inside and beat them. Then police say prisoner try to run away.' Joanna remembers the note George gave her in French. Taking it out of her draw she handed it to Mai. When she saw the green snake at the bottom of the paper, she dropped it as if the snake had bitten her.'

Joanna's flat

'Where was George?' Mai didn't give Joanna time to answer Rita.

'He's in a pit with the king of all snakes.' Joanna spoke.

'Mai said he was with king snake who lived in a pit. That wasn't all of it; Autile ran racketeering and gambling; he owned two casinos and most nightclubs. All his clients were diplomats, businessmen and the military. His pride and joy were the Sapphire Club. One of the many myths around him was that he had a golden bed that only his wealthy clients could afford to be entertained on. Rita looked at her watch.

'Is that the time? I'm sorry I'll have to go. Will you promise me you'll look at the leaflet for the residential home? I'll bring some shopping in on Thursday; you can tell me where George was. Your story's better than anything on the TV.'

Thursday morning.

Joanna and Rita listened to the news on the radio.

'This is the BBC news; rioting has broken out in many cities around the country. The worst of which was in Toxteth Liverpool. Police reinforcements from as far as Yorkshire had to be drafted in to help. Several buildings have been set on fire as running battles took place. Many police officers have been injured.'

'All these riots are taking the shine off Charles and Diana's wedding. Mai would be so excited about a Prince marrying a Princess. She would ask if they have a gold carriage and if the prince would bring his sword if a dragon turns up.' Mai giggles and speaks.

'After he kills a dragon, will they live in a castle and keep chickens.' Laughing, Joanna said.

'If Mai had her way, Buckingham Place would have hundreds of chickens running about.' Rita joined in the fun.

'That's one sight I'd love to see.' Joanna remarked.

'The Queen and Prince Phillip must be over the moon; Charles has found his true love. She is beautiful; I bet he can't believe his luck. He's thirty-two, and she's twenty; that's a good age gap. George was twenty-six years older than me. I watched the pawnbroker's window get smashed last night as they all ran in helping themselves; mind you, most of the stuff in there probably belong to them. I thought I was back in Shanghai.' Joanna looked at the sideboard. Standing, she walked over to the window. 'You can see the gate I always walked through on a Sunday after mass; there's a burnt-out police car there now. On the far side is the bench George and I sat on eating ice creams.'

'I had to leave my car on the other side of the park; the police have blocked off the roads. There was broken glass everywhere, Rita said. Then Mai spoke.

'Japanese will bomb the city; everyone must hide.'
'Mai would tell us to hide if the Japanese turn up and drop bombs. All these people are rioting what's gone wrong.' Rita thought for a moment, then explained.
'I suppose it's been coming for some time. No jobs, lack of opportunity, unemployment, poor housing. Many people in the black community feel like the police are targeting them; granted, there is a drug problem in the city, but they are in the minority and yet suffer the most.' Mai spoke.
'It's green snake he pays police.' Joanna answered.
'It feels like the green snake is in Liverpool.'
'This green snake person you were telling me about, what did George say.'
'He came back the day after Autile called.'

Shanghai.
There were reports of murders and buildings burning. Everyone blamed the students; some insurance companies blamed failing businesses for bogus claims. English newspapers asked everyone to remain calm and carry on as usual. Refugees from the north started to gather in the city, saying they had been forced from their lands. Finally, George turned up with his hand bandaged.
 'Oh! It's nothing, darling. I tripped up inspecting the troops.' He sat eating breakfast. Joanna looked at him and the dark lines under his eyes.
 'You had a phone call yesterday from a man; he said his name was Autile.' George kept reading the newspaper.
 'He's a local businessman stout fellow. I'll catch up with him later.' Joanna wanted to ask him if they were in danger and that he'd paid for their meal, and he'd killed a thousand people, but Madam Chung was busy eavesdropping. How could she explain her day out with Mai instead? She sat in silence. George continued. 'there's a party arranged for next week, one of those black-tie events, put that pretty dress you had on for the Colonel's birthday.' She thought for a moment and remembering the freedom she felt going to the restaurant she didn't ask him she told him.

'I'm going on a picnic today; some of the women from the bridge club have arranged to meet in the park.' She felt good at telling a lie. He didn't look up from his paper as he said.

'That's good, darling.'

'I'll be taking the maid with me.' She wanted to say I'll be with the only person I love who means everything; her name is Mai.

'I'm sure you'll have a great time.'

Joanna asked Mai to make up a picnic basket.

'Mistress, what did Madam Chung say?' Mai was shocked.

'Nothing, she just stood there. I think because I didn't ask for permission, she couldn't answer; putting your foot down felt good.' Mai was confused.

'Why you put the foot down? Did you squash a bug?' Joanna hugged Mai and kissed her, saying.

'What would I do without you.'

Joanna carried an umbrella to shield her from the sun. Mai was holding the picnic basket, walking two paces behind. Joanna kept stopping as she wanted Mai to walk beside her; also, she tried to carry the basket; Mai kept saying, 'not look good' The road led to a park not much dissimilar to the park in Liverpool. It had a boating lake, a bandstand and English Tea rooms. Mature trees swayed in the warm summer breeze. Further along, the road was the spot where the Chinese businessmen were assassinated. For a brief moment, the horror of that night made her stop.

'Mistress, what wrong.'

'I'm OK, so let's look for a quiet place to rest.'

Walking past the bandstand, a small regimental band played a selection of military marches. A few hundred deck chairs formed a semicircle populated mainly by British people. A sign hanging on the railings of the boating lake said, Shanghai Model Boat Club. There were no children, just by the lake, but men, some uniformly comparing the boats' size and speed. The path turns sharply, reviling small bushes leading to tall shade trees. They found an ideal place not overlooked and private. Kneeling up facing each other, they ate in silence, smiling all the time, occasionally laughing as they had escaped again. Laying down next to each other, Joanna held her hand as they pointed out clouds with shapes of animals or flowers. Looking around to ensure no one could see them, they kissed each other passionately.

'Poppy, you naughty dog, come back now.' It was a man's voice that broke their embrace. The small Jack Russell helped its self their sandwiches. Joanna rushed to button up her dress; as he walked through the bush, Mai pushed her shirt into her trousers. He was in a Captains uniform, pausing for a moment as he looked at them and spoke.

'I'm dreadfully sorry she's only a pup. I hope she didn't spoil your picnic.' Mai started to pack the basket away.

'No, it's no-fuss; we were just leaving.' The captain gazed at Joanna for a few moments, then said.

'I must introduce myself, Captain Crawford. I didn't catch your name;' he said this as if he was suspicious.

'Mrs Joanna Barlow.'

'Ah! Your George Barlow's wife. Well, I'm sorry if I intruded on your meal; good day.' The dog barked at them as she disappeared. Mai asked.

'Was he watching us?' Joanna thought for a moment, then said.

'I don't care, we've come here for a picnic, and we are going to enjoy ourselves.' Further in the park, they came across a beautiful lake; sitting on a fishing peg, they dangled their feet in the water, swans glided across to them. Joanna took leftover sandwiches out of the basket and started feeding them. Mai joked.

'I wish I was a swan. I paddle down the river and peck my brother's bottoms when they are bad.' Laughing, Joanna replied.

'I'd go looking for Captain Crawford's dog and peck its tail.' As the sun began its journey into the night, tired, they made their way home. Joanna wanted to hold Mai's hand, but that would be a bridge too far. At the crossroads, they would turn right towards the house. Three policemen stood in the way. Looking over their shoulders, they could see a car on fire, and a body was lying in the road. Directing them to move on, they had to go a long way home. The newspaper the next day reported another killing. The summer heat became intense and impossible to sleep; they lay in each other's arms.

'Tell me the story of the King and the spider. I like that one.' Telling Mai a story was an adventure in itself, as halfway through, she would get excited and mix the story up, making it sound better than the real story.

'Well, there was a king called Robert the Bruce who had lost a battle. He was sitting watching a spider spin its web.' Mai interrupted.

'His pet spider was a great worrier and said don't give up. Did he keep the spider in his pocket when he fights? In China, spider bite kill was the king of all spiders.' Joanna was still giggling as she fell asleep. Mai would usually climb out the window at dawn before Madam Chung caught them; this morning, it was eight o'clock, the phone ringing woke them. Joanna dressed quickly.

'Mai, stay here and polish or sort clothes out; she won't suspect us if you look busy.' There was no sign of Madam Chung as she picked the phone up.

'Can I speak to George, please?' Joanna recognised the voice.

'I'm sorry he isn't here at the moment.'

'If and when he is available, tell him to ring me.' He sounded angry.

'Who shall I say called.'

'Captain Crawford.' The phone went dead. Joanna's head spun. Was he going to tell him he caught her and Mai? in the park, running back up to her room, she tried to think of a hundred excuses to tell George, one being a wasp was inside her dress, and Mai helped to get it out, back in her bedroom there was no sign of Mai. Looking down into the garden see saw her talking to the gardener and kitchen maid. Mai ran back into the house to Joanna.

'Mistress terrible news. The burning car we see was the shit face. Students kill him. Madam Chung hides in a bottle very drunk.'

'Why would they do that.'

'Big secret says his father was Japanese.'

The knock on the door made them jump; it was George.

'I assume you've heard the news about Madam Chung's brother. Terrible business things might get a bit sticky around here, best if you don't go out. Sorry about the short notice, the black-tie party has been re-arranged for tonight. The car will pick you up at eight.'

'Won't you be with me?' Joanna had forgotten the wasp in the dress scenario; the bruises under his left eye drew her attention. He hesitated to reply.

'I. . erm...have to arrange a few things. I'll meet you there.' Joanna placed the dress on her bed. Holding her hands out to Mai to sit with her, she said.

'When this is over, we could get a boat like your family, fall asleep under the stars and be together.'

'Mistress, that would be wonderful. We could play tricks on my brothers and listen to my mother sing little ones to sleep. If Japanese come, we sail downriver to find a happy place.'

Joanna dressed in silence then sat as Mai did her hair. After putting her makeup on, she sat Mai down and returned the favour; their mood lightened. Mai kept sneezing as Joanna powered her face. Hugging each other for what seemed ages, Joanna made her way to the car. Confused for a moment, she wondered why a Rolls Royce was waiting for her. In the back was an ice bucket with a bottle of champagne in it. The driver wasn't the normal one; this one was English; he had a Welsh accent. Broad and muscular with the boxer's nose.

'Right then, tuck into the booze to get you in the party mood.' His leering grin sent a shiver up her spine—the streets were quiet, just the odd person walking quickly. George hadn't told her where the event was taking place as they headed out of town; soon, they were in a rundown district. Houses in a poor state leaning against each other avoid falling. He kept looking at her in the rear-view mirror, licking his lips. Eventually, they turned onto an industrial estate. A large building lit up by searchlights had a sign flashing in red, The Sapphire Club. Joanna's heart sank; she remembered what Mai told her about the green snake. The car slowed to join a traffic jam. On either side of the road, cars are parked. She gazed at groups of men in black suits, happily sharing conversation as they made their way towards the club. She wondered why there was no woman. That's when she saw him; Alister, George's drunken friend, was standing with a group of men, some of them drinking what looked like bottles of wine. Panic set in as she tried to open the door; it was locked; the driver just grinned at her.

Further down the road, what looked like fireworks lit up the sky. Two cars flew up in the air as they exploded, shattering the windscreen of their vehicle. The driver instantly reversed as he turned to see where he was going; blood trickled down his face. The sound of the plane defended her as it flew past, followed by another plane, and for a brief moment, she saw it drop a bomb on the club. A giant red ball billowed into the sky as the walls fell in, a third plane dropped its bomb outside the remains of the club. Still reversing backwards, the driver ran over someone; the sickening bumps knocked over the ice bucket. Men ran past most of their clothes, torn to shreds covered in blood, falling desperate to escape. One poor victim who was on fire fell to the ground motionless. The driver didn't speak as he drove fast along empty streets. The windscreen has gone allowing cool air to fill the car, yet the panic in her chest stopped her screaming. Through gasps in her voice, she called.

'Let me out now.' She tried the door again.

'No, I'll take you back to the house.' Holding a handkerchief to his face as blood seeped through. Joanna picked up the bottle, determined to defend herself. The car stopped turning to her, he said.

'Get lost.' Joanna jumped out, falling up the steps; she heard the car speed away. Safely in the hall with the house in silence, her screaming echoed in every room; Mai almost knocked her over as she hugged her, struggling to breathe, her arm felt heavy; when she saw the shard of glass sticking out and blood dripping on her dress, everything went black.

Joanna's flat.

'Oh my god, that's awful. That must have been horrible.' Joanna lifted her sleeve and pointed to a scar.

'Mai and the gardener patched me up. The Japanese blamed the Chinese, who said it wasn't them. Sometimes, when I'm

asleep, I think I hear an explosion for a few moments. I'm back in that car. The memory of that poor man on fire still haunts me.'
'What happened to George was he in the club.'
'No, he wasn't, but I never saw him again. Everything turns for the worse. The Japanese pushed into the city from the north; open warfare in the streets. Every day more and more people poured into Shanghai escaping the invasion. I found a letter from the army that gave George information on the safe zones, the international settlement, and the protected area, asking him to pack as soon as possible. I had no intention of going.' Mai climbs off the sideboard and stands behind Joanna, and speaks.

'I tell mistress to go she is safe; I go to my people stay on the boat.' Joanna listens for a moment.

'Mai begged me to go, she tried to convince me it would all go away and we'd meet again. I was selfish should have listened to her; nothing could separate us. The next few days, we didn't move. Madam Chung was still grieving; the gardener and the kitchen maid lounged about in the garden smoking. Mai and I just enjoyed each other. Occasionally we would jump, hearing gunfire in the distance. Then Captain Crawford turned up.'

Shanghai
'I hope you don't mind me calling without an appointment, but I must speak to you on an urgent matter.' Her stomach turned over, but she was determined to stick to the wasp story.

'No, not at all; what urgent matter.' She pointed him towards the main sitting room.

'Well, I don't want to alarm you, but the situation looks terrible. The Japanese have taken over half the city; also, I need to speak to George. Have you seen him?'

'No, I haven't. I was on my way to the Sapphire Club when the bombs dropped. He was to meet me there. I don't know if he's dead or alive.' She said this without emotion.

'Well, I can reassure you he wasn't there; he turned up at the officer's club the following day, quite drunk. He only stayed for a few moments then left.' 'Thank god he's alive.' She tried to sound relieved.

'The problem is he hasn't carried out any of his duties for some time. When was the last time you saw him?'

'He came to tell me to get ready for the black-tie party; that was the night of the bombing. I were so lucky had we arrived earlier, then I wouldn't be here. He'd arranged a car to pick me up.'

'I'm afraid George has been running up lots of debts; there are i.o.u everywhere. Mrs Barlow, I'll get to the point George will be court-martialled in his absence. Has anyone had contact with him?'

'Yes, a Man called Autile has been trying to speak to him. Do you know this man?' The captain walked backwards and forwards, thinking for a moment, then he said.

'You'll have to move out of this house; you'll be safe in the British zone. When the time comes, I'll send someone to move you; as for George, if he's done business with Autile, then God helps him.'

'What will happen to Mai and the other people.'

'Don't concern yourself about them as long as your safe. Once the Japanese get here, their fate will fall into their hands. Getting you to the safe zone, that's all we are concerned about.' Joanna became angry.

'I'm afraid I won't abandon Mai and her people. I won't be going to any safe zone.' His face became red as he started shouting.

'Good God! Woman, don't you understand what's happening. Have you any idea what the Japanese will do to you if they find you. Leave your pet thing and go to the safe zone. This dalliance you've been having with the scullery maid is disgusting.' As he said this, she abandoned the wasp.

'How dare you say that I love her? Anything you say or do won't change that. I'd sooner take my chances with the Japanese than go with you. Now get out.'

Mai stood at the top of the stairs as she watched the captain slam the door.

'Mistress captain is right; you must go.' Joanna sat on the bottom stair as Mai sat next to her.

'If I go, I might never see you again. I couldn't bear that.' Mai gently took her hand and led her back to the bedroom.

Joanna's flat

Rita put the shopping away and checked that Joanna had been eating.

'Have you had any breakfast?'

'No, I'm not very hungry. Just a cup of tea will do.'

'Too late, I've put sausages on the pan.'

'My mother makes sausages always on a Sunday. She makes extra for my father and brothers.' Mai said.

'Mai said it was her favourite.' Joanna looked at the sideboard.

'Have you looked at the brochure for residential homes? I'm sure you'd like them. I could take you in my car and have a view of them.' Carrying two plates in, she handed one to Joanna. Later as they sat drinking tea, Joanna said.

'I watched one of the buildings on fire last night. I think it was the dance hall. It brought all those memories from the Japanese bombing. Not surprisingly, the pub and post office were left untouched everyone needs money and a pint.'

'It's worrying riots are taking place all over the country. Last night, Mrs Thatcher was on TV; I'm not sure she's making it worse.' Rita rolled her eyes. Mai spoke.

'This woman sounds like Madam Chung. Is she Chinese?' Joanna smiled and then said.

'Mai would think Thatcher was related to Madam Chung,'

'You were telling me about safe zones in Shanghai. Did you go there?'

'Not straight away.'

Shanghai.

They saw Madam Chung, apart from the occasional collapse and drunken wail, the gardener and kitchen maid would carry her to her room. The weather became more intense with no break from the oppressive heat; every window in the house opened to catch a breeze. It was early morning when they heard the voices in the garden. Bleary-eyed, they crept over to the window; the scene below shocked them. At least twenty Chinese soldiers had assembled in the garden. Some lay badly wounded, others propped up exhausted against the wall. Mai joined the kitchen maid in the garden, talking to an officer. Joanna watched Mai run back into the house.

'Mistress, we have to help soldiers; need bandages, water medicine.'

Opening cupboards, they grabbed bedsheets and towels. The gardener filled a buck with water and carried cups and glasses to the soldiers. The officer pleaded with Joanna to help a medic do his best to stop a soldier from bleeding to death. Hesitating for a moment, she knelt as he made her close the wound, blood oozing onto her hands quickly; he stitches it up. Mai leaned against a tree, holding a soldier with a hole in his chest; gasping for breath, he slid to the ground and lay motionless; there was nothing she could do. They did their best to help; four died in the garden. The officer spoke to Mai as they picked up their dead comrades and carried them away. Joanna understood some of what he was saying. Burn all your clothes with blood on them; they will execute you if the Japanese find you helped. Later the gardener burnt the last of the evidence, making sure he put extra dry wood and leaves on the fire; bits of ash floated into the air, remnants of a tragedy as the sun weakened. Although the night they could hear gunfire, sometimes in the distance than close by making them jump. Mai woke early to make breakfast; she was met at the bottom of the stairs by the gardener and kitchen maid. They told her that Madam Chung had left in the night.

'Mistress, she has gone Madam Chung gone take lots of things. She like a thief in the night' Joanna sat up in bed.

'What did she take?'

'She leaves two spoons, two forks, two knives, take everything else; also, gardener and kitchen maid leave later go back to their people we are alone.'

'Mai, what will we do.' Mai walked over to the bed and spoke.

'White Kingfisher, show us the way.'

Joanna's flat
'It sounds like you were in hell. How did you cope?'
'We had each other that's all that matters, the following day; all the electricity went off. Mai went out and managed to get enough food for a few days. We found candles and made hot food in an old fireplace. The fighting had stopped for a while. The plan was we'd hide in the attic if the Japanese turned up; after that, we settled down, staying in the bedroom.' Mai spoke.
'We light lots of candles made funny shapes on the wall; Mistress make a rabbit I make a dragon.'
'Mai and I would make shapes on the wall in the candlelight.'
'Did anyone check on you? Surely the army could help.'
'I did get a call from the liaison officer to say that they wouldn't pick me up; I'd have to make my way to the British zone. Then someone from the officer's club called asking for George, he sounded angry. The days passed; we were happy in our little world. We even played hide and seek; Mai was excellent as she knew all the best places.' Mai giggled as she spoke.
'Mistress scream when I surprise her.'
'It's a wonder the Japanese didn't hear us; I did scream a lot when Mai jumped out on me. Then more and more gunfire could be heard, we watched Japanese planes fly over the house, and moments later you listened to the explosions. The best time to go out at was night, although it was still dangerous. Mai had to go further searching for food while she was out; he came.'

Shanghai
Joanna was tidying clothes they'd dried that day; with her back turned, she heard the bedroom door close. Turning, she expected to see Mai. He dressed in a white suit, tall and slim; his face smooth with a small moustache, hair black and slicked back.
'Who the hell are you get out.' Joanna screamed. He walked over to her dressing table.
'Please accept my apologies. I should have made an appointment 'enchante mademoiselle'. My name is Hanri

Autile.' Picking up an ornament and inspecting it as if browsing in a shop. 'Your husband has a business arrangement with me.'

'I don't care who you are; get out; George will be back any moment.'

'I'm afraid George is currently residing at one of my establishments.' He sat on a chair and looked in the mirror, smoothing his hair with his hand.

'I'll call the police, now get out!' Backing away towards the window, she started to shake.

'I think you'll find the police are, shall we say otherwise, engaged with our Japanese friends. First, before we get down to business, can you tell me what you know of George. There must be questions you'd like to ask. I can fill in all the missing details. You see, I know so much about him. Ask yourself why he never slept with you.'

'How dare you? I'll call for help.' Laughing, he removed his coat, placing it carefully over the chair.

'George has worked for me many years, apart from his duties he is also one of my best customers along with the British establishment. My brothels are very diverse and provide a comprehensive menu of delights. He has eclectic tastes; his appetite for boys is insatiable; the younger, the better, his mistress is opium. Unfortunately, this puts him in debt. As you know, debts have to be settled. You're not the first wife he's brought to me. He's very good at picking ripe ones ready for plucking, if you'll excuse the pun—my requirements where they had to be young, white and virgin. You fit the bill perfectly. Ask yourself how long George observed you in your park; when the time was right, he pounced. Ask yourself who paid for the ship bringing you to Shanghai or how he could afford to live in a house this big. The British Army never asked questions as it would compromise their horizontal entertainment.

'None of that's true, for God's sake, get out!' Sobbing, she begged him to leave her alone. Taking his waistcoat off, he continued.

'The truth can be hard to take, but I owe it to you as you enter my service. Everything would have gone like clockwork had the bombs not dropped. You were 'The Pot' on the night. It's a simple arrangement of ten tables with five players playing poker. A thousand dollars just to sit down, the winner from each table plays on with the others until there is an eventual winner. That's when they get you 'The Pot'. The losers get to watch as the winner samples first prize. I provide a bed in the middle of the club; everyone gets a good view. After they have finished well, you belong to me. A white English woman brings me a considerable profit. Even the Japanese officers will pay extra. Sadly, it all went up in smoke. That brings me to why I need some reward for all my labour. Take off all your clothes and lay on the bed, and please kick, scratch and scream; you'll enhance my pleasure.'

'Don't you come near me; do you hear get out?' She picked up a footstool to defend herself. He grabbed the stool and threw it out the window as he walked towards her, picking her up by her waist; they landed on the bed; ripping her clothes off, she bit him on his hand. Smiling, he said.

'Ah! Yes, that's more like it.' Joanna heard the crack as he seemed to go rigid. Pulling away from her, she saw Mai holding a small bronze ornament. Blood trickled down his back. Grabbing Mai by the neck, he started to strangle her. Falling from the bed, Joanna crawled across the floor and picked up the ornament. Swaying for a moment, as she stood, she struck him. His skull burst opens his knees buckled as he hit the floor motionless.

Joanna's flat.
Rita sat opened mouthed, then she said.
'You killed him.' Mai speaks.
'We kill green snake all Shanghai do celebration dance.'
'Mai wanted to do a celebration dance. We sat on the bed for two hours, looking at his lifeless body. Mai walked over to him and kicked him; he didn't move. We were in shock; then it dawned on us we had to get rid of him. Mai had noticed his car parked on the corner; She ran back out to check if anyone was there; the road was empty. We helped each other put his jacket on him then dragged him down the stairs. We had to keep stopping as it was exhausting. Eventually, we sat him behind the

wheel; she took the handbrake off and let it roll down the hill towards the main road where all the trams went into the Bund. It seemed to take forever before it crashed into a tree. Another dead body on the streets of Shanghai was part of life now.'
'What did you do then.' Rita didn't blink as she spoke.
'We went back into the house. He'd bled out into a rug, so we rolled it up the following day set fire to it. The funny thing was I had just killed another human being and felt nothing. Even now, I have no regrets.'
'No one would blame you. It was self-defence.'
'I started panicking, unable to breathe. The whole world came crashing down on me in an avalanche of emotions. Images in my mind, the park, my mother and father, and George bought me ice cream. A sickening feeling in my stomach, I was an item not genuine, not human. I was violently ill, vomiting and gasping for breath. Mai clung to me; how could George be so cruel I was happy with my life. My whole existence was a joke. At that moment, if I didn't have Mai, I would have killed myself. I had no remorse over killing Autile, yet I sympathised with that poor man on fire at the club. He was part of that hideous night; what would have happened to me if the bombs hadn't dropped. Would the man who, in some ways, I mourn for have abused me had he won? I was so innocent when I met George. I had no voice coerced into a vile plan. There was no authority I could go to for justice; I just had to be glad I was alive. We lived in the attic; if his people came looking for him, no one came. Mai was able to get a newspaper; the article announced Autiles death as a tragic accident; it even called him a local businessman. One morning we watched the Chinese and Japanese fight a running battle outside the house. We had to duck as stray bullets smashed through the windows. As the fighting stopped both sides retreating, the phone rang.'

Shanghai
They looked at it ringing, frightened to pick it up. Slowly Joanna answered it.
'Hello.'
'Joanna, why are you still in the house.' It was Monique.

'Monique, oh! Monique, thank God!' Joanna sobbed, 'Thank God we don't know what to do. Can you help us? He attacked us . . . we. . had to . . . oh! God. . .'

'Slow down; why didn't you go to the British zone. Where is George.'

'They wouldn't let Mai come with me. I don't know where he is.' There was a pause before Monique spoke.

'You need to get to the French zone; both of you can stay with me. Let me give you my phone number and address, vingt-huit Avenue de septembre. How soon can you come?'

'We could come tonight. We'll start packing now.' The sense of relief at hearing her voice was overwhelming. Monique cautioned her.

'Only take what you need; you'll have to travel light; they have started shooting looters.'

After the phone call, Joanna and Mai raced up the stairs. They sat on the bed one hour later and looked at four suitcases. Opening them, they painstakingly sorted what they could down to two, then one.

'Mistress, what about the sideboard?'

'We can't take it with us.'

'White Kingfisher, keep us safe. My brother has a cart he helps us.' Joanna shook her head as she spoke.

'No, Mai, just leave it.'

'Bad luck if we don't take.' Joanna couldn't argue with her.'

'Very well, we'll take it.' Mai ran out of the house.

Sitting alone, she looked around the bedroom, remembering the first time she kissed Mai. Her gaze took in the White Kingfisher on the sideboard.

Joanna's flat.

Joanna went quiet for a moment staring at the sideboard, Mai kneeling at her feet.

'Mia seemed to be gone ages; I started to worry as the light faded. What would become of us? I started thinking, what if I hadn't gone into the park that day? Would George have picked someone else? According to Autile, he was meticulous in his planning? How many other girls did he have on his list who met his requirements? I realised that there were only two people in my life, Mai and Monique. I know what you're thinking; what about my mother and father. I felt they were complicit; my mother was only interested in what the neighbours would say; my father was a simple man who thought he was doing me a favour.'

'I understand how you felt, but they tried the best for you.' Rita sympathised with them.

'Look how it turned out.' Mai speaks.

'They make a big mistake, but they love you.' Joanna stared down as if she was looking into Mai's face.

'Mai would say they did it out of love.' Rita looked at her watch and spoke.

'Do you know what? I don't have to rush off today. How about I make us some tea.'

Later as Rita washed the dishes, she drew Joanna back to the story.

'Did Mai come back with her brother?'

'Yes, by then, it was dark. It didn't take us long to put the sideboard on the cart. We stood for a while at the front, looking back at the house. Then we moved; the streets were empty, just the occasional burst of gunfire. Monique's house was about two miles away. A Japanese soldier hung on a lamp post with a sign on his neck at the corner of Victoria Road. It said, 'no prisoners. It didn't take us long before we got to the French zone as the names of the roads changed to boulevards and Grande rue. At the crossroads, we could see a sign saying Avenue de septembre. In the distance, I caught sight of Monique waving. Just before we crossed, a Chinese army wagon stopped; soldiers climbed out and surrounded us, demanding to know where we were going. Mai spoke to them and pointed to me. She told them I was a French Diplomat, and they were helping me move the French zone, urging me to keep walking; followed by her brother, she asked for news about the Japanese. They relaxed and started smoking.' Joanna stopped talking. Rita realised how emotional her story was, and reliving it was painful.

'Would you like me to get you a drink?' Joanna shook her head.

'The wagon burst into flames knocking them to the ground, and The Japanese scored a direct hit.'

Shanghai
Joanna stood frozen for a moment; then, she ran towards Mai, kneeling with her lifeless body. Sobbing, she pleaded.
'Mai! Mai! Get up; we've got to go. Monique's waiting, Mai, please, we can go to Liverpool and keep chickens.' Joanna tried to get Mai to put her arm around her shoulder; it just fell. She started kissing her face. 'Please, my love, please speak to me; you can't die; I won't let you the white kingfisher will help us.' Joanna was unaware of the burnt and twisted bodies of the Chinese soldiers lying close to her. A second bomb landed on the other side of the burning wagon. The blast knocked her away from Mai. Unconscious, Joanna was carried away by soldiers and local people. Monique guided them to her house, where they placed her on a kitchen table. The blast had torn half her clothes off, losing blood from a wound at the back of her head; small pieces of shrapnel peppered her leg; Joanna was slowly slipping away. Monique made frantic phone calls for help. Heavy fighting around the hospital made it impossible to call an ambulance. Eventually, she found a French surgeon through the embassy. He didn't expect her to survive but set about stopping the bleeding.
'I can't do any more for her. She needs a blood transfusion.' Monique asked.
'Where can she get it?' The surgeon replied.
'We can do it here. My blood wouldn't help; I'm diabetic. Do you have any health issues?'
After retrieving a medical case from his car, Monique sat at the table with her arm on a pillow as the tube turned red. The surgeon kept checking Joanna's blood pressure; it wasn't good, but now he'd stopped the bleeding, she stood a chance. Connecting the drip to her arm, he spoke.
'All we can do now is pray.'
'How much blood does she need.' Monique said, desperate for it to work.
'She has no internal bleeding, so two pints should be enough; it's hard to say she is in shock.'

The hours seemed to pass at a snail's pace. The surgeon urged her to get some rest. She would have none of it; gently stroking Joanna's head, with a shawl around her shoulders, she fell asleep. Daylight burst through the windows as Monique woke with a start. The surgeon reassured her that Joanna was no longer in danger as he sat drinking coffee at the table.

'We moved her into the bedroom. I'm happy with her, but some of the shrapnel will be in her leg for life. When she wakes, I'm afraid the trauma she has been through will need as much help as possible. Not just Joanna, how are you after witnessing the attack. If you need to talk, just call me.' Monique answered.

'I haven't had time to think about it; if I do, I'll fall apart. I'll keep focused on Joanna; thank you for saving her life.' Smiling for a moment, he replied.

'Your blood saved her life.'

After he left, Monique remembered; all the letters Joanna sent her told of Mai and how much she loved her and their adventures. She thought of her Phillip and how she never got to say goodbye. She felt she had learned to get over the pain of losing him, but her heart found a room full of grief and sorrow; it took most of the day for her to compose herself. Mai's brother called the next day; the housekeeper translated for her. Mai's family had already moved upriver to escape the Japanese. He told them that Mai would be buried in her grandmother's village. He had a small box in his hand with braided strands of Mai's hair as a keepsake; her family thanked Joanna for her kindness to Mai. Monique remembered one of Joanna's letters where she said Mai wore a yellow dress when they visited a hotel on the Bund. The dress was in her suitcase, neatly folded. Monique said it was Mai's favourite dress. The housekeeper spoke for a while with the brother. He gently took it off her; he left with tears in his eyes. Mai would be buried wearing the yellow dress. The next few days, Joanna slipped in and out of consciousness. Monique spooned water into her mouth. If she did wake for a moment, the look of horror in her eyes, her whole body shook before she passed out. Monique was an early riser, but this morning after a difficult night nursing her, she slept on; the clock in the hall struck eleven; in a panic, she raced to her bedroom. The bed was empty. Had Joanna died in the night, and they didn't tell her. Looking out the window, she saw her sitting in the garden on a bench.

'I can see her face when I close my eyes.' looking straight ahead, she said. 'Why didn't you let me die.' Monique sat next to her.

'Then I would have lost my best friend.'

'This pain I have will never go away. How can I live without her? Tell me how can I live. It's my fault that Mai died. I should have stopped her.' Monique took her hand and held it tight.

'Mai would want you to live. Although I never met her, your letters told me all I needed to know. She was funny, loyal and in love. When I lost Phillip, nothing mattered anymore. In one of his letters, he said that I must not ignore the world's beauty if anything happened to him. If I see the sunrise, he will see it or the glorious colour of a flower, then they will see it together. He said our love added up to something that would grow. His words were the only thing that saved me. It's not enough to say I know what you're going through; these words sound hollow. What I can offer you are my friendship and love.' There was a pillow and a blanket on the bench. Monique placed the pillow on her lap; Joanna rested her head as Monique wrapped her in the blanket. The following day after breakfast. Monique gave her the box with Mai's hair.

'I thought I'd wait until you were stronger. You'd been through so much now is the time to tell you. Mai's brother came with it as a thank you from Mai's family. I gave him the yellow dress she wore on the big adventure. Mai was buried in the dress.' Joanna could not speak but mouthing the words with eyes full of tears.

'Thank you.'

The fighting continued in Shanghai day after day, with more reports of killings and massacres. Joanna's injuries began to heal. The surgeon made his last visit to her as he returned to French. Happy with her recovery, he was concerned about how much weight she had lost. As he left, he said.

'la nourriture est le meilleur remede. Joanna answered him in English.

'I promise never to leave an empty plate. I can't thank you enough for saving my life.'

'I did what I do best, but without Monique's blood, I'm afraid the outcome would have been different.' This hit Joanna like a thunderbolt. After he left, she asked Monique.

'You gave me your blood.' Monique tried to dismiss the question.

'It was nothing.' Joanna held her arms out to her as they cried together. 'Your half Jewish now you'll have to start going to the synagogue.' For the first time, Joanna laughed.

The phone rang one morning; Captain Crawford asked to see Joanna. She said no at first, but Monique told her he had urgent news for her. The few occasions Joanna met him didn't go well, but as he walked into the living room, his body language was different, his voice full of concern. Joanna sat in the window seat; she asked him to sit, but he said he'd prefer to stand. Monique joined them and sat next to her.

'How are you? I trust you're well cared for; I'm afraid I have some bad news. George has been killed.' Joanna half expected him to say this.

'How was he killed?'

'He was fighting behind enemy lines. He died a heroic death defending the empire.' There was no mention of Autile or the brothel. 'Rest assured; we will hunt down the enemy and bring them to justice.' Joanna wanted to say, don't bother; we've already seen to him. 'I know this is a shock, and we all pass on our condolences. There have been many donations to the widow's fund, and the woman's guild is organising a charity event. The proceeds will go to you and help provide financial help as you try to rebuild your life. I'll call the other day with some paperwork making it easy for you to claim your army widow's pension. In the meantime, the officers club had a collection; I have an envelope with five hundred pounds for you as you'll have expenses in the days ahead.'

As he spoke, Joanna stopped paying attention. Closing her eyes for a moment, she could see Mai's face smiling, saying.

'He full of the shit bull.' She wanted to giggle; Mai always mixed-up sayings, then back into the room in time to hear him say.

'Stout fellow and a credit to the regiment.' News of George's death had no meaning to her. For a brief moment, she could see the stranger in the boating lake rescuing the little boy's boat. 'George will have a full military funeral. He upheld all the fine traditions of the British army, and we are truly thankful for his sacrifice.'

Joanna's flat.
Rita sounded angry when she said.
 'But none of that is true?'
 'Well, think about it they didn't want a scandal, and every story has a hero. Captain Crawford was eager to talk money as somehow, I would keep quiet, and it all goes away.'
 'What happened to George.'
 'His naked body was found in an alleyway. With Autile gone, someone else took over; they had no use for him. How could I tell the truth he was a national hero now?'
 'How long did you stay in Shanghai.' Rita called from the kitchen, making a pot of tea.
 'I never wanted to come home; I wanted to go to Mai's village and die there; the fighting got worse. Captain Crawford arranged passage for me back home. A ship sailing to Hong Kong was our last chance. Monique was able to go with me; we shared a cabin only as far as Marseille; at least we were together.'

Shanghai.
Their suitcases packed, they waited for a car to take them to the port. A British army staff car arrived at nine-thirty in the morning, followed by a small removal van. A Sargent driver explained that the Japanese now controlled Shanghai and agreed on safe passage to the harbour and the Bund. He wasn't allowed to carry a sidearm. The Union Jack fluttered at the car's front opposite a white flag. They had to have their papers with them for inspection. The journey to the Bund would have taken forty minutes, but they had to stop at many roadblocks. The last part

of the journey took them past Joanna's old house. In disbelief, they gazed at a burnt-out building destroyed. The driver explained that Chinese soldiers had occupied it, two Japanese planes ended their occupancy. Memories of the house flashed through her mind, Mai's first kiss, lying next to each other, and the desperate fight for life with Autile. They turned onto the hill where they pushed Autils car and down to the tramlines that took them on their big adventure. The tree where Autile crashed had marks of the impact.

In the distance, more blockades. Stopping at one of them, they were outside the Metropole Hotel, all its windows smashed. It seemed only a few days ago when she and Mai had lunch. Smiling to herself, she remembers a tipsy Mai saying, 'my people in the big boat with money.' Eventually, after a tense standoff with two Japanese soldiers saved by Joanna speaking in Chinese. They demanded to know what was in the removal van. When they opened it, looking at the sideboard, they asked for proof of purchase, explaining that anyone caught looting would be killed. Joanna remembers she placed it in a draw, climbing in the back; she started rummaging about Mai sitting on top of it, watching her as she spoke.

'Mistress, I put it in a book.' Joanna paused for a moment as she remembered Mai putting it there.

'Ah! Her it is.' She handed it to the soldiers, who seemed annoyed they couldn't shoot her.

As the ship left its moorings, she stood on the deck and looked at a war-torn city. Gone was the vibrant noise, the busy workers calling each other, the sound of ships horns echoing across the bay. The smell of flowers from the small boats replaced with burning timbers and the pungent smell of cordite from the bombings. There were no horses, only barbed wire and soldiers everywhere. Joanna slept the first few days; she would dream about holding Mai and wake up screaming at night. Monique would hold her until the terror passed. Other nights Joanna would sit on the deck, unable to sleep with the shrapnel aching in her leg. Monique read some of the letters she'd received from her family in France and Germany each day; the Nazi's were beating people up, mainly Jews, laws were passed every week restricting all Jews movement.

'I'd arranged to close all the shops. One letter from my cousin complained that I was too rash that all this political stuff would soon stop. He had both legs broken on his way home from the synagogue.'

'I don't understand why are they so cruel.' Monique looked at Joanna; even though she had been through so much tragedy, she was still young.

'I'm afraid I'll have to start bribing people to get my family out of Germany. I don't care if I lose it all as long as they are safe. One of my relations managed to send his two young daughters to America; it cost him three thousand dollars for the paperwork.'

The bond between them was profound. Monique always had the right words, always quietly listening. They had shared so much with each other that the thought of her leaving the ship depressed Joanna. As if she was reading her mind, Monique spoke to her as they sat on the deck.

'It's going to be difficult leaving you at Marseille. Will you be alright?'

'I wish I could come with you.' Joanna looked at her in the hope she would say yes.

'What will you do when you get home.'

'I can't face my parents, not yet. I'll stay in a hotel for a while after that rent a house.' When Joanna sailed from Liverpool, each mile was slow; now, she felt the ship was too fast.

Singapore.

Monique and Joanna went ashore for a few hours to post some letters and pick up mail; Monique had a private mailbox in every port. Walking past a newsstand, Monique came to a halt and grabbed a paper. The headline said, 'Germany invade Austria.'

'Dear God, no!'

'What's happened.' They found a park bench and read the newspaper repeatedly; sadly, the story didn't change. Monique sat staring into the distance.

'This will make things so difficult. I just hope they leave the banks alone long enough to move my money.'
'What will you do?'
'Move it all to Monaco. From there, I can start making arrangements.' Looking at Joanna and taking her hand, she said.
'I'm afraid the world is changing so fast. Things will never be the same.'
They sat shaded by tall trees. Mai was feeding her strawberries, a gramophone playing next to them, 'keep young and beautiful.' and Major Crawford's dog asleep on a blanket. Mai speaks.
'When strawberries are gone, we look for wasp.'
She woke with fright as the cabin door opened. Monique carried a tray with food and drinks in.
'You were in such a deep sleep; I didn't want to wake you. It would have been a shame as you were smiling.'
'What time is it?'
'Ten thirty, you've missed breakfast; we still need to keep your strength up; by the way, what were you dreaming about.'
Joanna grinned.
'Something nice.'
Before they left for Bombay, Monique received news from a contact in Berlin that the German government were considering all Jews who have property and savings over five thousand Reichsmarks must declare it.
'What does it, men.' Joanna asked.
'They want us to do an audit of our wealth, so they know how much to take off us.'

Bombay
It was a different world from Shanghai. No sign of war, just a city at work. Joanna sat outside the telegraph office while Monique franticly sent telegrams. Watching the people go by, she thought of Mai. They would have lived together in China if things had been different. She wanted to cry, but for a moment, she imagined what Mai would say; 'sadness is a big black bird that don't feed it.' As they walked, Monique said.

'From now on, only send your letters to my private post box's. They have started intercepting the mail.' Her mood changed, smiling, she said. 'We only have a few hours before we sail; let's lunch in the best hotel, drink champagne, and raise our glasses to Mai. We'll have oysters with a mignonette sauce followed by caviar.'

'That would be lovely.' Joanna hugged her. 'Let's invite Mai; she would love it.'

They sat in the hotel restaurant where Joanna modelled the jewellery. The waiter set the table for three and filled three glasses. Monique suggested a toast.

'To Mai, whose family have lots of money in the big boat.' They both laughed and clinked their glasses. Mai laughed with them. When the waiter served the oysters, she looked at them.

'Oysters good, my mother say smell like the wind from the sea.' Joanna paused for a moment, then said.

'Mai told me you could tell a good oyster by its smell.'

Joanna's flat

Rita had to knock a few times before Joanna woke up.

'I've got your prescription and some shopping. The doctor said that he'd like to call and see you one day this week. He's concerned you haven't followed up on your appointment with the hospital.'

She dismissed the question.

'I don't know what all the fuss is about; I'm fine; all the meals you've made me have got me back on my feet.'

'I'll come with you to the hospital If you want. You can tell me all about sailing back to England last time you'd left Bombay.'

'The last part of the journey was dreadful; the closer we got to Marseille; I would lose the only person who kept me sane. I asked Monique we'd only talk in French for the last part of the journey once I get to Liverpool; there be no one to speak the language.' Rita made breakfast as they sat eating, she asked.

'When it came time to say goodbye, it must have been painful.'

'More than you'll ever know.'

Marseille.
The ship was in port for two days; they often walked without saying anything. After lighting candles in the Cathedral, they sat for a few moments, then Monique took off her engagement ring and gave it to Joanna.

'I want you to have this, Phillip and I would love you to have it.' Shocked, Joanna shook her head.

'No! No! I couldn't take it.'

'I want you to have it; I have no one to give it to.'

'What about your family? Can't you give to one of them?' Monique placed the ring in her hand and held it with both hands.

'I'm afraid I'll never see them again; anyway, we are blood relatives now. If we come through this, I'll come to Liverpool, and you can give it back to me. Je penserai a toi tous les jours porter l'anneau.' Joanna answered in English.

'And I will think of you and keep it safe..'
Walking back the to the ship, they stopped for a moment at the café they sat in on the first voyage and had two Singapore slings. For a short time, they laughed at funny moments they spent together, none more when Joanna modelled the jewellery in Bombay

'That poor man couldn't take his eyes off you. Fortunately, he bought more than he needed.' Joanna laughed then said.

'He asked you was I your daughter.' Monique gazed at her for a moment.

'Oh! If that was true.'
A car with her luggage waited on the quayside for Monique as they said their goodbye's, hugging each other for a few moments, unable to speak, the call came to board the ship broke their embrace. Monique waited as the boat slipped its moorings. Joanna watched her walk along the quayside for a while, waving, turning she was gone. The cabin felt so lonely as she sat on her bed; Monique left an envelope on her pillow.

My Dera Friend

'I will never forget you; I believe Phillip is with me always, Mai is with you. There is an old saying; It's not looking at each other in love that matters; it's looking in the same direction.

Au revoir mon doux amour. Monique

Joanna's flat.

'The rest of the journey was difficult. People tried to make conversation, but I did my best to avoid them. I'd read every book on the ship when the news came through the Germans' and partitioned the Sudetenland. I heard one of the passengers say give Hitler an inch, and he'll want the world. At that time, all I knew was that the Jews were persecuted; another guest said Mr Chamberlain would watch him. Hitler wouldn't take on the British Empire; send a gunboat, and they'll run to the hills.'

'When you arrived home, what did you do.'

'Sailing up the Mersey didn't feel like coming home. I recognised the buildings, but it was a city of strangers. I only had a few possessions, the largest being the sideboard. I'd arranged to put it into storage. I took a taxi to the Adelphi hotel. Walking through the doors reminded me of the hotel in Bombay; it had the same grandeur. My room was palatial with a chandelier and beautiful velvet curtains. My first evening there was a welcome surprise, the waiter who served me was French, although I did get him into trouble as I kept him talking too long the head waiter started serving me. I think he thought I had designs on him.'

Rita called from the kitchen

'Cheese on toast nearly ready.' As she prepared the food, Joanna called to her.

'You know the sideboard saved my life during the blitz. The air raid shelter was always full; I had to sit outside and watch the Luftwaffe, so I climbed under it the next time they visited Liverpool and took my chances. That's when all the windows blew out. The blast knocked the wind out of me as plaster fell, landing on top of it. When I went outside, the air raid shelter was gone, just a big hole in the road, all those poor people.'

'That sideboard must be your good luck charm.'

'I'm afraid it isn't.' Rita placed a cup of tea next to Joanna.

'We've only got skimmed milk.' Mai laughed at this.

'Best milk straight from cow nice and warm.' Joanna smiled as she remembered.

'Mai would always say warm milk from the cow make a happy drink.'

Liverpool 1938.
She breakfasted early and decided to go for a walk. Eventually, taking her past the shipping office she used to work for, some of her colleagues were standing outside talking, didn't notice the well-dressed woman passing by, stopping at a newsstand; the headlines shocked her. *GERMAN DAY OF WRECKING AND LOOTING. Synagogues Burned Down in Many Cities.* Wrapping her fingers around Monique's engagement ring, she said a silent prayer. When she arrived back at the hotel, she asked could the daily newspapers be delivered to her room first thing every day; when the receptionist asked her which newspaper, she said all of them. One morning she saw an advertisement and wondered why she hadn't thought of it before. *Chinese Laundry Park Street reasonable prices next day pick up.* The hotel had its laundry, but it could be a chance to speak to someone in Chinese. Walking as fast as she could, she headed to Chinatown. Placing a small bundle on the counter and rang a bell. A young man walked in and spoke in English.

'Hello, we charge by the weight, that okay.' The look of shock on his face as she spoke Chinese.

'I'm okay with that. Your advert said next day pick up can it be done sooner.'

'I tell my grandfather, please wait.' An older man in his eighties walked in wearing a long black silk coat.

'There is a café across the road; my grandson will come to you when it's ready. Can I ask where you learn to speak Chinese?'

'I lived in Shanghai. I've just arrived in Liverpool.' Smiling at her, he said.

'It's a pleasure to meet you, a lady from Shanghai; I'm Zhang Whi.'

'Joanna Barlow pleased to meet you.'

The café was small with cane chairs and plastic tablecloths; The walls had large paintings of the Chinese countryside. Joanna felt at home; she ordered soup and a pot of tea. Then, she started a conversation about the weather with an older woman who seemed confused and then told Joanna how the damp weather made her bones ache. Speaking Chinese felt like freedom. She did trip over a few words but settled. Suddenly a crowd had assembled outside, all of them curiously looking at Joanna through the window. Zhang Whi pushed his way through the crowd and walked in, asking could he sit by her as he had a few questions speaking only in Chinese.

'There are many people outside who have family in Shanghai. We get newspapers, but people who are suspicious of them think they are lies. They want to talk to you.' Joanna felt panic for a moment then said.

'I couldn't talk to all of them; I don't know what to say.'

'I go outside pick one or two; the rest have to wait.'

The first to come in was a man and a woman. They had a son who was a student; they hadn't heard from him. Joanna had to be careful not to upset them. 'As I was leaving, lots of people moved west to escape the Japanese. The students did protest a lot; all the people in Shanghai supported them.' They asked her whether she had heard his name; she answered no. Next was a man whose brother was in the Chinese army. She told him about the heavy fighting in the city and them retreating into the countryside. More and more people desperate for news came in, but as it took her three months to travel home, things would have changed. They started calling out the names of roads; 'Nanking Road, my sister, worked in a book shop her name is Lian, another called out 'My brother work in hospital his name Xiu Ying.'

I'm sorry I don't know them.' She could feel the desperation for news. A woman in her fifties pushed past everyone; she held a copy of 'Da gong boa' Chinese newspaper that was three months old.

'It says green snake dead is it true.' Joanna looked at the photograph of Autile and, for a moment, felt he was in the café, had his murder caught up with her.

'Yes, it's true.'

'How do you know it's not a lie.'

'Because I saw his dead body. His skull was split open.' There was a gasp from the crowd then they all cheered. Joanna felt overwhelmed by it all. Had she sailed home, or was she still in

Shanghai. Zhang Whi asked them all to leave then shut the café door.

'You saw his body; where did you see it?'

'He was in a car accident.' He could tell she knew more

'The green snake had people here in our community; two young girls went missing, their family in debt to him, taken back made to work in his brothels, and paid off the debt. We found out the people who did this; they had contact with the British army.'

Joanna wanted to run out of the café. Was this contact George? Did he help take these young girls to Shanghai?

'What happened to Autils people.' Zhang Whi, unblinking, said.

'They were dealt with.' She felt a shiver, looking at an ornate sword in a case above the door. She knew he could sense she was holding back, looking deep into her eyes, for a moment, she could hear Mai's voice, 'tell him the truth.'

'I killed him.' She blurted it out. 'He attacked me. Mai and I put him in his car and pushed him down a hill.'.

'You don't have to tell me anymore, I believe you. This Mai you speak of, where is she.'

'The Japanese killed her. I survived.' Her voice was full of emotion. 'Her family were boat people; they lived on the Bund.'

'You have a great love for Mai.'

'She was everything to me; I wish I died with her.'

'I won't ask you why Autil attacked you; it's not important.' Smiling, he stood and went into the back of the café. Joanna looked at all the faces looking back at her through the window. He placed a bottle of brandy and two glasses on the table. Then put a silk ribbon around her neck, multicoloured with small diamonds sewn into it. There was a gasp from the crowd outside, the sound of people talking excitedly.

'That ribbon is only given to great warriors; it's called Xiang Yu's ribbon most sacred. The Qin army persecuted my ancient people; The warlord Xiang Yu defeated him save our people; only a great brave warrior can be given the ribbon from then on. You have earned that honour. We are forever grateful to you. One of those girls was my granddaughter.'

'I'm so sorry what happened to her.' Smiling, he said.

'They are safe now; we also have a long reach. The man responsible an army officer was dealt with.' This hit her hard; picking up her glass, she drank the brandy in one gulp—the thought of George laying naked in a back ally. For a few moments, she couldn't comprehend the enormity of what had happened and how connected to all of it she was. Sitting in front of her was the man who arranged George's death. 'You are welcome here anytime; please don't be a stranger.' Standing, he took both her hands and bowed his head. 'There is a saying leave slowly return quickly.'

Walking outside, the crowd went quiet, all smiling; stepping sideways, they created a corridor; at the end was an older woman; Joanna later found out she was a hundred. Leaning on a walking stick, she approached her, touching the ribbon she said.

'I see the shadow of the white kingfisher with you. You are blessed.'

On the way back to the hotel, she stopped, unable to breathe, leaning against a wall; she wept a few people asked her was alright; back in her room, she collapsed on the bed and slept.

Joanna's flat.

'Oh! My God, that's incredible; what are the chances of that happening. Did you go back to Chinatown?'

'Yes, many times, they were always suspicious of officialdom and bureaucracy, so whenever they received important letters, I would translate if they didn't like the content; it didn't matter they trusted me. I sat many times with Zhang Whi sharing a meal or a drink; we never spoke of Autile; I knew he knew more. The funny thing was I had a nickname they called me the Shanghai Lady; It did sound a bit dubious, but I loved it, so I became a regular visitor. On Wednesday, I would go to a bakeshop run by Annchi Liu; she was a lovely woman who told the filthiest jokes. Her pies and cakes were delicious; I even helped her daughter deliver her baby, a girl. She'd gone into labour in the kitchen. After all, I'd been through, seeing new life gave me hope. They wanted to call her after me, but I asked them to call her Mai. There were so many times when I forgot I was in Liverpool. Chinatown was my refuge, a sanctuary where I was accepted.

Rita sipped on a cup of tea and asked.

'Had you heard from Monique?'

'No, her letters just stopped, then I read all Jewish gold and precious metals, silver and diamonds, had to be handed over to the German State. Can you imagine what that would do to her business? She had my address, so all I could think of they were just delayed. I found a modest house to rent not far from my parents. I had every intention of going back to China when the political situation changed. I'd been back six months and hadn't visited them. My mother didn't recognise me at first. She said I looked older. I couldn't tell her about Mai or what I'd been through; I was a widow grieving for George, the hero. My father had lost his job through poor health; I was shocked he looked so frail. I didn't stay long. I took two hundred and fifty pounds out of the bank and returned the next day. It was a small fortune then enough to see them through. I did write occasionally, but I never saw them again.'

'What did you do after that.'

'The war broke out.'

Liverpool 1941 the May blitz.

They sat on chairs outside the air-raid shelter listening to the sound of explosions in the distance.

'I can't see the point of sitting outside of the shelter.' The woman had said this more than once. Joanna sarcastically replied

'Well, Mrs Jackson's five children could swap places with you, should I ask her.'

'No, I don't mean that; why don't they make them bigger?'

'Write to the war office I'm sure they'll accommodate you.'

The heavy drone of the Luftwaffe planes flew above them, illuminated by searchlights, their night's work of death and destruction over. The all-clear sounded everyone made their way home. Joanna cooked breakfast, then fell asleep in the chair, with Mai watching from the sideboard. *Dreaming, she stood at a tram stop in Shanghai, looking at her watch, wondering where Mai was. Then she noticed Autile's car against the tree. The grandfather from the laundry sat next to him smiling; he looked at her, saying her family have money in a big boat.'* The sound of the air raid siren woke her; she'd slept all day. Determined not to sit outdoors again, she lay under the sideboard. The first explosion was the closest they'd experienced, the second even closer. The whole house shook as part of the ceiling crashed onto the sideboard; a moment later, the windows blew in, showering the room with glass. A red glow instantly lighted the front room, opening the front door; half the houses opposite were gone, the rest on fire. Hobbling over rubble, she looked for the air-raid shelter; all that remained was a hole in the ground. A man called to her for help. Half buried; a young girl trapped under a wooden beam. Lifting the beam together, she crawled out covered in blood. Joanna carried her to her house and lay her on the sofa. Not realising she was in shock, Joanna felt faint for a moment and knelt on the floor. Mai spoke.

'Mistress, get sheets and water; don't let Japanese find that you help them.' Speaking to herself, she said.

'I need water and sheets.' The man who helped her then carried an older woman in and sat her in the chair; she was holding a scarf to her head as blood trickled down her face. Joanna called to the man.

'We must work fast; the Japanese will be here soon. We must burn all the evidence.'

'What are you talking about, love? It's the Germans who are dropping the bombs.'

Her house filled up with more wounded people. Joanna cut up sheets and gave as much first aid as she could. A policeman and St. Johns first aid appeared at the door; two nurses quickly supervised their removal to the hospital.

'Who did these bandages.' The nurse said as she checked them.

'I did; it was all I could do.' Exhausted, she sat on a chair.

'Well, you did a first-class job; we could do with more people like you.'

Joanna sat in the corner of the church hall as nuns handed out mugs of tea. That's when she saw Mrs Jackson sitting with her five children. The man who helped lift the wooden beam sat next to her.

'The Jackson's had a lucky escape; the shelter was full, didn't she only go to one a few streets away, thank God.' Joanna thought about the woman who complained and wondered if she had sent her letter to the war office. Against all advice, she went back to her house; the next few days, local people helped make the places left standing habitable; the windows were intact at the back of the house, giving some daylight. A nurse from St John's Ambulance called one morning.

'I'd thought you'd like to know the young girl you rescued has pulled through. You did a brilliant job.'

'Thank God!' Joanna took her into the back kitchen and made a cup of tea.

'Would you consider joining the service; we are desperately short of first aiders.'

'I haven't done any training.' The nurse handed her a first aid book.

'Read that ask quickly as possible.' She then handed her a first aid kit armband and a steel helmet. 'The church hall is a temporary dressing station. We assemble there at four this afternoon.'

Joanna's flat.

'The next three nights, the Germans throw everything at us. We couldn't keep up with the casualties; whole roads disappeared. Then a maternity hospital took a direct hit; when we got there, the police told us there was nothing we could do. I'd seen so much death and destruction; I was only in my early twenties, but what I witnessed that night, no one should ever see.' Mai spoke softly.

'I hold you when you sleep.'

'I couldn't get the images out of my head; I dreamt Mai was holding me, and at times I thought Mai was lying next to me; this helped me sleep; I would dream of Monique and hear her voice soft reassuring me. Then one night, we had the raid from hell. Hundreds of incendiary bombs fell, the church near Chinatown was hit first, then Annchi Liu shop. Frantically digging through the rubble, they found her; placing her on a door, they carried her to Zhang Whi's shop. We did our best to save her, but it wasn't enough; she died.' Rita asked.

'How did you cope? I can't imagine how bad it must have been. How did you get through in one piece?'

'Looking back, I didn't care for myself; If I were killed, then I would be with Mai. People got us through, drawing strength from each other, looking out for each other, surviving from day to day. After Annchi Liu's funeral, everyone got drunk then repeated her most filthy jokes. I wet myself laughing. The war changed; the bombs stopped then the Americans turned up. Slowly we emerged towards normality, granted there were shortages. We felt the war would end when two American soldiers, second-generation Chinese, came into Zhang Whi's café; unfortunately, they only spoke English. Zhang Whi shook his head, saying, 'how can this be someone has stolen their tongue.' That was when I received a letter from Monique.' Joanna opened a drawer and took out an envelope. 'It's in French, so I'll read it.

My dear friend, I hope this finds you well; I'm in Vianna trying to get one of my cousins across the border to Switzerland, but there is no more jewellery left. I fear the people helping me will expose me. I often think of you and our voyage to China; I know Mai is with you always. If I come through this by some chance, we'll go to Singapore, get very drunk, and behave disgracefully. Remember we are 'soeurs unies et sang'

Monique

'What did that mean?' Rita asked. Joanna folded the letter and placed it back in the drawer.

'It means sisters united in blood. I tried for years to find out what happened to her then in nineteen fifty; I received a letter from the French embassy, they were very accommodating, Monique's cousin did escape to Switzerland. Unfortunately, Gestapo found her; they took her to a concentration camp.'

'Oh my God, no. Joanna, I'm so sorry. I thought she would have survived.'

'It seems one of the neighbours informed on her. I have memory, and happy moments we spent together and did not think about what happened to her. My heart aches for her even now;

how unfair it was. I can still see that beautiful woman who put sun cream on my neck the first time we met and how she held me when I woke to scream in the night. It took me a long time to get over her death. Where ever I go, trouble followed me.'
'What do you mean.' Rita asked.
'The war took so many lives the pain of the survivors would be a lifelong torment. The poor man who lived next door came home with the weight of the world on his shoulders and seven letters. That's when I ran headfirst into the Catholic church.

Liverpool 1943
'Another bloody false alarm. The Germans ran out of bombs ages ago. That's the last time I'll go in that stupid shelter. What's the point? I'd be better off sleeping under that sideboard with you.' Joanna made a cup of tea and placed it in front of her neighbour.
'There you go, Winnie, that will cheer you up.' Mai lay across the sideboard laughing. Joanna smiled as she informed Winnie.
'My friend Mai would like you; you'd make her laugh.'
'Does she live locally?' Joanna paused for a moment.
'No, she is in Shanghai waiting for me.' Mai sat up, saying.
'I never leave you.'
'Have you heard anything from Frank?' Joanna asked.
'No, I haven't. I've still got the Christmas tree up with his presents. When he comes home, I'll do a big roast. I've even managed to get three bottles of stout that will put a smile on his face.'
'Why couldn't he come home on leave.'
'Essential maintenance, they said, he's the only one in the whole of the royal navy who can fix a leaking pipe, doesn't make sense?'
Joanna notices the shadow of a figure moving past her window; looking out; she sees a telegraph boy gazing around.
'There's a telegraph boy in the street.' With panic in her voice, Winnie said.
'Dear God, no, don't say that, which house is he looking at?'
'He's just looking around.'
'Sweet Jesus, please not my house.' Joanna had to tell her.

'Winnie, he's outside your house.' Winnie began praying.
'Dear God in heaven not my Frank, please not my Frank.'
Joanna opened the door and spoke to him. He handed her two brown envelopes and said he was sorry. People in the street stood to attention as the sight of the telegraph boy only meant terrible news.

'They're both addressed to you, Winnie.' Frozen in fear, unable to speak, she nodded when Joanna asked if she could open them, reading the first aloud.

'Hi, Love. Got Shore Leave at last. Coming home stuck in Bristol, be with you Sunday. I'll ring the Rose and Crown at two o'clock Saturday. Love Frank.'

Winnie let out a scream and sank to her knees, thanking God. Joanna opened the second one.

'The Admiralty regrets to inform you that Frank Brennan has been killed missing in action.' That's all it said. It doesn't make sense.' Winnie was angry.

'Tell him to come back. He's got the wrong house. Please give it back to him; call him back; he's given us two telegrams; ask him what's he playing at.'

A loud knock on the door made them jump. It was Lilly Jackson crying, holding a telegram.'

'The Egret has been sunk; I've lost my Bert.' Joanna caught her as she collapsed. In the distance, she could hear people crying out as the young telegraph boy delivered more envelopes.

Joanna's Flat.

'What was the Egret?' Rita asked.

'They called it the Liverpool ship. Frank was one of many local lads who served on it. They all went to the same school and played in the same football teams. In just three streets, six men went down on the ship. The burden of surviving was too much for him. What made the situation worse he had six letters from his mates. They would censor any mail in those days in case the Germans intercepted them, but the lads stuffed them in his kitbag.'

'What did he do with them?'

'That's when I met Father Maguire.' Mai spoke.

'Holy man, powerful, I don't like him; he has God with two people and a chicken.'

'Mai would tell me to be careful watch out for holy magic. As for the letters, they became a divisive weapon for the church.'

Liverpool 1943

'The whole street wants to pass on their condolences; what should I do.' Joanna was looking out the window. 'They keep knocking.'

'I can't face them. How can I tell them Frank wasn't on the ship?

'They'll find out soon enough on Sunday. You have to tell them.' Another knock on the door but this time, it was a priest. Father Maguire, thin-faced haggard-looking, spoke with a soft Irish accent; dust-covered, he apologised.

'I'm sorry for the way I look. I had to crawl under rubble to give a poor man the last rites. Winnie, the whole parish mourns with you and all the other families. It's unimaginable the pain you must be going through. Is there anything I can do? Would you like to pray?' Winnie, frozen to her chair, looked at Joanna to tell him the news.

'Frank wasn't on the ship; he was allowed shore leave. He'll be here on Sunday.'

'Holy mother of God, that's fantastic news.' Winnie found her voice.

'That's why the Christmas tree is still up. His presents have been waiting for him.' Winnie started crying.

'Would you like a cup of tea.' Joanna asked both of them. While she was out of the room, she could hear them talking. Winnie is unable to open the door. The priest is happy to spread the good news. Joanna thought what kind of reception this news would bring, for many no comfort at all. Joanna had only met Father Maguire once before; she assumed he was doubtful of her, asking, I haven't seen you in church. Her answer, 'I'm afraid God and I no longer talk, I took him to Shanghai and left him there.' set the tone. Winne went into hiding, spending most days in Joanna's kitchen; this only worsened as some of her neighbours became suspicious. While standing in a queue,

Joanna overheard a conversation accusing Winnie of hiding something, and Frank somehow knew the ship would sink, so he jumped ship to save his skin.

'Please come with me on Saturday.' Winnie begged her.

'Of course, I will; you'll be fine.' Joanna imagined a frosty reception at the pub, judging by the gossip in the street. 'Isn't there a phone further away he could use?' Winnie shook her head.

'No, it's too late; I just want to hear his voice tell him I love him.' Mai spoke.

'He knows she loves him, his voice always in her head it called song without words.' Joanna smiled for a moment then reassured her.

'I have a friend in Shanghai; she would say the song of love without words always in your head. Whenever I miss her, I close my eyes, and I can hear her sweet voice.'

Saturday, Winnie clung to Joanna's arm as they walked to the pub. No one spoke to them, but the only sound was children playing in bomb-damaged houses, smashing remains of any windows. The manager was an old friend of Franks greeting Winnie with a hug, then directing them to a small corridor behind the bar. The phone was on a table with two chairs.

'What time will he call.' The manager asked.

'Two o'clock.' Winnie replied with tears in her eyes.

'Well then, I'll make you a cuppa or would you two like something stronger.' Before they could answer, the phone rang. It was as if a bomb had gone off; they all jumped. Hands shaking, she picked up the receiver.

'Is that you, Winnie.'

'Yes, oh Frank, thank God. Where are you?'

'Stuck in Birmingham, lots of damage on the track.' There was a long pause, then Franks voice full of emotion broke as he sobbed. *'All the lads, Winnie, all the lads have gone!'*

'I know, my love, it's unbearable.'

'Little Jacko was the last to say goodbye, Christ he's got five kids. I can see them every time I close my eyes; what am I going to do? I don't know what to do. All my mates, I should be with them.'

'Don't say that just get home, love, come home; I'll see you Sunday.' The line went dead. The manager didn't make tea as he put two glasses of whisky in front of them. Walking back home, Father Maguire was waiting outside Winnie's house. Pulling Joanna into an entry, she begged her.
'Can we go to your house? I can't face him. He keeps asking me how I feel, and the church will see us through. He wants me to go to a special mass for all the men on the ship. How can I Frank wasn't on the ship, also have you seen the way people look at me, I can't take any more.' Walking up the back entries and into the kitchen, she kept looking behind her. Sitting by the fire, Winnie put her head back and fell asleep. The light began to fade as Joanna drew the curtains. Gazing at her neighbour, she wondered what she would do when Frank came home. She had a feeling of sorrow for both of them. The sound of breaking glass woke Winnie up.

Joanna's Flat.
'Why would someone smash Winnie's window?' Rita was shocked.
'They blamed Winnie and Frank for what happened. They were angry he survived.'
'But that's ridiculous; how could they.' Rita's protested. Mai spoke.
'My mother says anger a spice that spoil the pot.' Joanna smiled as she said.
'You know Mai always had a saying for everything; anger was a sour spice.'
'What happened when Frank came home.'
'We waited all day. Winnie walked up to the bus stop a few times; there was no sign of him, so we just sat there.'

Liverpool 1943.
They sat on either side of the fire in Winnie's kitchen, watching the flames, not saying a word. Joanna could feel Winnie's anguish with each sigh of mumbled prayer
'Where is he? He said he'd be home in the afternoon; it's ten-thirty oh! I hope something hasn't happened.'

'He'll be here soon; he did say bomb damage on the rail line. He just got delayed.' She had spent the day reassuring to no effect.

'Did you hear that someone's in the yard?' Opening the door, they could make out a figure by the coal bin. It was Frank dressed in his long navy coat and cap. He was holding his kitbag tight.

'Frank, it's Frank; oh, love, how long have you been there. Come in; why did you come the back way.' As she guided him into a chair, Joanna had seen the look on his face so many times in Shanghai he was traumatised with dark rings under his eyes, nothing like the wedding photographs over the mantelpiece happy and smiling. Winnie went to take his kit bag off him to make him comfortable, but he clung to it. He sat staring for a while as Winnie ran out of things to say.

'Take your coat off, love, let me help you. God, your freezing; how long were you were standing there.' Frank answered in a whisper.

'I'm not sure I can't remember; they're all in there, all of them in the kit bag. I can still hear them singing.' He wasn't making sense; the three of them sat for a while without saying a word. Winnie broke the silence.

'How do you feel now, love? Did the train come in late?'

'No.. .I walked for a while. I wanted it to be dark. Where's my kit bag.'

'Frank, you've got hold of it.'

Joanna knelt next to him, softly speaking.

'Frank, why don't you go to bed? we'll bring a cup of tea for you.' He didn't recognise her for a few moments, then nodded his head. Still clinging to the kitbag, he made his way up the stairs. Turning to Winne, she said.

'Give him the time he needs; he must be exhausted.'

'I'll do the Christmas roast tomorrow that I'll put him back in the pink.'

Realising that Winnie would need as much support as Frank, Joanna offered to make the dinner giving her time to care for him. The following day she let herself in to find Winnie still dressed and asleep in the chair; when she woke, she said Frank hadn't taken his coat off and was still holding the kitbag. A knock on the door surprised both of them. Winnie asked.

'Look out the window. If it is Father Maguire, don't open it.' It turned out to be the telegraph boy with another brown envelope.'

'It must be a mistake; he only came home last night; he can't go back.' Joanna reread it as Winnie paced up and down. It was a new posting he had seven days before reporting to a new ship in Belfast. 'Can't they give him a job in an office? He's very good with words, and his handwriting is beautiful.' They hadn't noticed him standing at the bottom of the stairs, without his coat but still carrying the kitbag. He spoke quietly.

'Seven days is an exception; normally, you only get three.' Both women, startled for a moment, sprang into action. Joanna raced to put the kettle on. Winne fluffed up some cushions as he settled in the chair. Winnie sat opposite.

'Is there anything you'd like me to get you, love?' He shook his head.

'I was in Bristol when I heard the ship had gone down, the train came and went I couldn't take it in. They were all laughing when I left; they'd given me a month's rum rations, I nearly fell off the ship.' He went quiet for a moment. 'They'd stuffed loads of letters in my bag; I'll get in trouble, I said to them if they find them. There in the bag all the lads. Winnie, I've lost all my mates.' He began to weep. 'I should be with them.'

'No, no, don't say that, love, your home now; the tree is still up your presents are ready to open. Joanna is making a roast.'

Later in the evening, Joanna sat opposite the sideboard. All the ingredients for a Christmas roast are uncooked in the kitchen. Winnie and Frank were fast asleep in their chairs when she left, presents still unwrapped under the tree.

'Mai, I wish you were here; you would know what to say.' Tiredness gently guided her to sleep, dreaming of Mai back in Shanghai, both wearing their dresses from the big adventure. They sat by the boating lake, watching the lonely swan cleaning its feathers. Mai tells her a story.

'When men go to sea, guardian fish always follow the ship. They have wings; people think they are birds when you see them.

They carry the spirit of souls lost to the sea on their backs to feel the wind and see the blue sky again; this makes them happy stops them from wondering the world lonely and in pain; it helps loved ones see them in their dreams.'

The following day Winnie sat with her head in her hands as Joanna let herself in asking.

'Where's Frank.' Winnie's face red with tears answered.

'He's still in bed; I've just read one of the letters, Joanna; it's unbelievable; I've put them back in his kit bag. My head was spinning; I couldn't look at them. I need to think. Thank God he's home. Why did he come in a back way? I hope he's going to be alright.' Her mind was racing.

'Winnie, slow down. Have you had breakfast you need to eat? I'll make you something we don't want you falling ill.'

Joanna noticed Father Maguire in the backyard.

'They keep giving me the third degree. I hope you don't mind me using the back door. Some of the bereaved families have asked to speak to Frank. I know it's difficult for all of you, but would he talk to them? After all, he was the last one to see the lads alive.'

'We'll have to wait and see, father. When the times are right, I'll ask him. He's got letters the lads planted in his kitbag; we've tried to read them, but it's too upsetting, and anyway, they are private and personal.' Father Maguire's face became severe asking.

'Where are these letters now?'

'Upstairs in his kit bag.'

'Can I see them?' He sounded angry; Joanna spoke up

'I think it's best to ask Frank first; he's asleep, so you'll have to come back.' He looked across at Winnie.

'Tell him to do nothing before I see him. Do you understand?' He left by the front door with a loud slam. They sat for a while. Winnie couldn't understand why the priest was so angry; she started to take the Christmas decorations down, sighing as she went. Joanna helped her then said.

'I don't think he'll give up until he talks to Frank about the letters. The families who want to talk to Frank could meet in my house if that helped.' Relieved, she replayed.

'Oh Joanna, are you sure? It's not a bother to you.'
'I'll make lots of scones; we could use some of your chairs. I think I have a bottle of whisky somewhere.' Winnie had a worried look on her face.
'What if they get angry and gang up on Frank.' Joanna reassured her.
'I think he'll be fine.'
Confessional in Our Lady of Sorrows. '
'How can I help?' Father Maguire asked as the door closed.
'Bless me, father, for I have. . .' Lilly Jackson didn't finish her sentence as she sobbed.
'Do not be afraid to tell me your troubles.' He reassured her.
'I don't know where to start; oh father, I can't take it anymore. I've lost him. What am I to do? My children who'll care for them.'
'The Church will help. The local community will help. God will see you through this. He will guide you.'
'How will he father how.?'
'God will provide. Take the sacraments to seek comfort in Jesus. The power of his healing love will help.' Lilly was more composed now and angry.
'Will it bring Tommy back. Will the children get their dad back? Why didn't God stop the ship from sinking?
'I can't answer these things or why they happen. Please don't turn away from God. You'll find comfort here.'
'I throw a brick through his window, and I'm glad.
'Who's window?'
'Frank's
'Why! Why! Would you do that?'
'Because that bastard survived and my Tommy didn't. He hasn't got children; I've got five. It's not right!'
'He hasn't done anything wrong. He was just lucky.'
'Why did God spare him? Why! God's cruel why didn't God think about my children.'
'We don't always understand Gods work, but we know he loves us.' He argued.

'Doesn't feel like love to me. I'm done with God.' The door of the confessional bang shut as she left.

The following day Father Maguire called early.

'I'm sorry to bother you, Winnie, but Frank's been back three days now. I hope to talk to him about those letters before he meets the families.'

'He won't talk about them. It's taken all his strength just to agree to meet them.'

'Well, if he's having problems with the letters, maybe I could take them.'

Joanna walked in from the kitchen to his annoyance, said.

'I don't think he's ready to do anything with them, father.' His answer said a lot about his intentions.

'I didn't know you were a spokesman for Frank.' Winnie defended her.

'I don't know what we would have done without Joanna; she's been a rock to us.' He looked at both of them for a few moments, then said.

'Promise me he won't tell the families about them. Do you understand?'

'I think that's up to Frank their all coming round tonight, so we'll see. I'll show you out.' His answer surprised both of them.

'You don't have to. I know where the front door is.'

At seven o'clock, a small crowd gathered outside Joanna's house, mothers and father's sisters and brothers and a little girl aged four who'd lost her uncle. Joanna welcomed them in.

'Please come in, Sit anywhere. I'll put the kettle on.' Frank sat in the backroom looking down at his hands clasped as Winnie took scones out of the oven. Frank stood up and spoke.

'I'll go in on my own.' Winnie disagreed.

'No love, I'll sit with you.' Frank shook his head; Joanna asked Winnie to help with the drinks. They listened for a while in the hall; they heard laughter after an awkward silence. Opening the door, Frank was entertaining them.

'So anyway, Petty Officer says, right, you'd better come and see the captain poor Robbo gets marched off to the captain, he says able semen Roberts reckons he can see Blackpool tower, Blackpool Tower, says the captain in Malta, he says, don't tell me the Germans have invaded Blackpool and brought it here. How do you reckon that he says? My binoculars says Robbo. I can see Blackpool Tower. It turns out the lens had a crack; he thought he could see the tower.' Robbo's mother spoke over the laughter

'What an idiot waits till I get my hands . . .' She paused and then started crying. Joanna offered her a plate.

'Here we are. Mavis, take a scone.' One of the men asked Frank.

'How were the lads when you left the boat

'They were in great spirits singing doing silly walks. Mind you; they got into a load of trouble a few weeks ago.'

'Why what happened?' Before he could respond, the little girl started laughing. Her mum told her to stop; her answer didn't make sense.

'The lady on the sideboard keeps making funny faces.' For a brief moment, they all looked at the sideboard. They wouldn't have seen Mai putting her finger to her lips. The little girl copied her and returned the wink.

'We'd gone the pub, and things were going well singing and that. Ronnie was playing the piano with half the keys missing. When a group of soldiers came into the Scottish regiment well in no time, it all kicked off; glasses and chairs were flying through the air. How tall is Mogsy?' John Copper, Mogsy's dad, answered

'He's about five foot five, I think.'

'Doesn't he pick up a six-foot Sargent and chuck him over the bar.' Proud of his son, his dad punched the air.

'Get in there, Mogsy!. The last time I spoke to him, he said he would train for the Longsdale Belt; he had a great left hook.' Mogsy's mum spoke up.

'What were they singing?'

'Wish me luck as you wave me goodbye. Maddox did that whistle thing that sounds like a strangled cat, then the rest of them started doing the Can-Can.'

Eventually, they started to leave everyone hugged Frank as they went, a few of the women cried as they held him. The little girl waved at Mai; unfortunately, Joanna missed her busying in the kitchen. Exhausted, Frank went to bed. The two women sat talking.

'He has these terrible nightmares. He jumps out of bed and grabs the pillow. I manage to calm him down. He thinks his pillow is his life jacket. He's not ready to go back on duty.' Joanna cautioned her.

'He has to. If he doesn't turn up, they'll send MP's and arrest him.'

'That's awful; there must be something they can do like a classroom where he could train up recruits.'

The following day Father Maguire called not the angry Father who slammed the door; he was friendly and enquiring

'How did it go last night?'

'It was a bit awkward at first, but then he told them some of the antics they got up to we had a right old laugh. It didn't take long before Frank had them singing.' Winnie hoped he wouldn't ask about the letters.

'That's good laughter is the best medicine, as they say. I've come to let you know that there will be a special mass for all the lads on Sunday. I was wondering if you are up to attending.' Winnie shook her head.

'I'm not sure, father. I don't know if our presence might be a distraction.'

'I know that he has a date to return to active service.'

'Yes, on the 24th he has to report to Belfast. It's wrong. Frank's been through enough. Can't you speak to someone father? They might listen to you.' He smiled as he said.

'Winnie, I wish I could then I would have to do it for many others; it wouldn't be fair. I was wondering if he'd decide on the letters. If he's going on the 24th, then there isn't much time left.' He looked at her intently.

'You know what, father, we'll just have to wait and see.'

'I need to talk to him about the letters; maybe we could spend some time together soon.' Joanna hadn't said anything, but she interrupted him.

'As soon as he decides, we'll let you know.' He bit his lip as both women stood up; without saying a word, he left.

Later in the day, they had an unexpected visitor. Joanna answered the door to see a policeman. He asked to see Winnie. Walking into the front room, she saw a familiar face.

'Hello, Winnie.' Bill Taylor went to school with Winnie; they played together as children.

'Hello, Bill.'

'Has something happened?' Joanna asked.

'Bill has come to see me.' Winnie had a worried look on her face.

'Why, what's happened? Is it something to do with Frank?' Bill spoke.

'I wonder if I could speak to Winnie alone.'

'It's alright. Bill, Joanna can stay; she needs to hear what you have to say.' The policeman puffed out his cheeks.

'Very well. I've had a report of an assault.' Surprised, Joanna said.

'Assault, what kind of assault?' Winnie pattered Joanna on the arm.

'Let Bill do his job.'

'At 11.30 am Yesterday in Norwood St, an altercation involving you. Mary McCormick says you punched her in the face knocking her to the ground.'

'Yes, that's right.' Still in shock, Joanna looked at her.

'My God, Winnie, what happened? He continued.

'She says that it was an unprovoked attack.'

'No, that bits wrong we had been arguing.'

'What was the argument about.' He hadn't taken his notebook out, just listening to her.

'Well, she approached me saying it wasn't fair her daughter has five kids and no father. She blamed Frank, saying he fiddled his way off the ship and was a coward.' Joanna defended her.

'How could she say that I'd knock her block off myself.'

'Is that when you hit her?'

'No, I tried to walk past her, but she said something.'

'What did she say?'

'She said I never deserved kids as I was as barren as the Sahara Desert. That's when I hit her.'

'Let's get this right; she verbally attacked you, and you thought she meant you harm, so you defended yourself.' Winnie nodded her head.

'That sounds about right; I'm glad I hit her; had she got up, I would have hit her again.'

'Look, I have to tell the Sargent at the station if this needs further action. I'll let him know that it was six of one and half a dozen of the other.'

'So? what happens now?

'Nothing! Mary McCormick is angry you can understand it her daughter Lilly's lost her husband, poor soul, five kids and no dad.' Relieved, Joanna said.

'So that's it then.'

'Yes! By the way, while I'm here, can I see Frank, this is the first chance I've had, and Winnie, don't go hitting anyone else.' Winnie guided him to the back room.

'I'll put the kettle on.'

Frank sat eyes closed by the fire. Looking up, he said.

'Hello, Bill, I haven't seen you in ages; come in sit down.'

'I was passing through I'd stop for a chat. How are you doing, mate.' Bill thought it best to say nothing about Winnie's fight.

'Not good. I am just hanging on. I'm still in a dream, keep thinking I'll wake up, and it didn't happen—Jesus Bill, all those lads. I can still hear them singing.'

'I wish I could say something, but words sound empty. Somehow you have to get through. Those lads led me a merry dance when I was a young copper. I remember running after them; no matter how hard I tried, you never caught them. I remember them laughing as they ran little buggers. Do you remember that time they went on the day trip to Wales?' Frank smiled.

'I was with them; they were full of devilment. That was the day they smuggled a sheep onto the coach.' Laughing Bill said.

'The coach driver had had enough and pulled up at the police station, didn't he? Can you remember their excuse why they were bringing it back?' Oh! Yes, they said it was lost, so they wanted to keep it as a pet. The fact that Jackson's dad was a butcher had nothing to do with it.' Winnie came into the room with some tea.'

'Here we go, Bill. I've put a bit of whisky in yours.'
'You'll get me the sack drinking on duty. Well, It's for the lad's cheers. God, that's strong. I won't be able to blow my whistle.' Frank looked into his drink for a while without speaking, then said.
'I don't know. I can hear the lads sometimes laughing, shouting, calling after me! The other day I went down to the river. I got on a ferry boat. I needed to be on the water again; give Winnie some space; she thought it was a good idea.
'How did that go?
'I was at the back of the boat looking at the wake in the surf. I leaned on the guard rail. I could hear them calling me. I don't know. . .' Shocked Bill said.
'What are they saying.'
'They say 'come on frank were all waiting' I started to climb over the rail.' Bill gulped on his drink.
'Good God, Frank! Tell me you didn't think about doing something stupid.'
'It just felt like I would be fine. I could keep an eye on them. Then this woman tapped me on the shoulder.'
'Thank God she did.'
'She asked me to hold her baby; the wheel had come off her pram. As I held the little thing, something happened.'
'What was that.'
'The little mite smiled at me. I cracked up and couldn't stop. The woman sat with me for a while. We didn't say much she seemed to know. Then I got off that boat and came home.' Bill offered him some homespun advice.
'My mother used to say, 'you never know when an angle will turn up. I don't know, but why don't you talk to the lads? It might help.'
'Winnie will think I'm mad
'I don't know; If I could talk to them, I'd say Mogsy if I get my hands on you, I'll lock you up. What do you think he'd say.' Laughing, Frank replied.
'He'd say, 'If he had two broken legs, I still wouldn't be able to catch him.'

'That's it; Frank, don't be frightened to talk to them if you do! Tell them I said the next time I find them playing pitch and toss, I'll put them in front of a hanging judge.'

'Thanks, Bill, you're a good man.'

'Well, I'll have to go. I've got to find a missing dog and a side of beef. Finding the meat will be easy.' Curious Frank asked 'How do you reckon that?

'Wait until they start to cook it. Just follow the smell.'

Joanna and Winnie had been listening from the kitchen. Joanna whispered to Winne as Bill left.

'It's a pity Bill couldn't join the navy; keep an eye on Frank. He didn't say anything about your fight.' Winnie changed the subject.

'You don't think there's a problem with Father Maguire over these letters, do you? He seems to get angry about them.' The two women sat with Frank, Winnie asked him.

'What do you want to do about the service on Sunday.'

'Can you and Joanna go if anyone asks? Just say I'm unwell.'

Our Lady of Sorrows Church, Sunday.

'Normally, at this time, I would be talking about the Holy Spirit, this would be Wisdom, Counsel and Fortitude, but today's mass is about the lads as we always refer to them. I baptised all of the lads, gave them their first communion, guided them through confirmation and watched them grow into fine young men. I'm heartbroken for the families and can only wonder at the pain and sorrow they have to endure as more pain falls from the sky night after night forcing us to regroup and pick each other up. It feels like there is no comfort, but they were together when they gave their lives protecting all of us. That much we know. Now we must band together in Christ and continue their fight.'

'It was a lovely service. Frank, the church was overflowing. Farther Maguire gave an excellent sermon; I think the whole congregation wept.

'I'm glad you went. I couldn't have faced it.'

'So many people came up to me and asked about you. While we were outside, Father Maguire asked me if he could call to see you tomorrow.'

'I'm afraid it's the letters. I don't know what to do.'

'You can't leave it any longer; love, it's wearing you out.
'I want to keep them, not let anyone have them.' Joanna sat opposite asking.
'Frank, why do you think it's so hard to pass them on.'
'Because I can hear them talking to me. I have to let the lads go if I let the letters go. Some of them leaned on my back as they wrote them; I can still feel that, hear them laughing all my mates.' He started to sob.
'Come on, love; we'll do whatever you want. Don't be upsetting yourself. Put your head back and try and have a nap. Joanna, fetch the blanket.' They settled him down then went into Joanna's house

'He's fast asleep. What do you think he should do with the letters?' Winnie looked at her, sighing as she said.

'We should have posted them anonymously when he first came home, nobody would have known, but they have become attached to him he can't let go. It's awful, and now Father Maguire seems to be making it worse; it's a terrible burden he is shouldering. That man sitting in the chair isn't my Frank. I want my Frank back.' Mai speaks.

'Tell lady how you full of pain in Shanghai how you learned to see the sky feel the wind on your face. My mother says flowers always turn to kiss the sun.' Joanna sat next to Winne and took her hand.

'Winnie, you still have Frank. Whatever it is that's giving him so much pain, you'll find a way. I lost the most beautiful person in Shanghai; I held her in my arms as she slipped away. The one thing that saved me was a friend who gave me her blood. I never thought I'd live again, but I did; Mai would have a saying for any situation; she would say that flowers always turn to kiss the sun. I miss her every day, and yet my love for her keeps me going.'

The following day Father Maguire called. Joanna guided him to the back room. He didn't acknowledge her as he walked past her. She wondered how much pressure he would have put on them had she not been there. Winnie greeted him.

'Hello, father, please come in, sit down, would you like a drink.'

'Yes, a cup of tea will do fine, thank you. Hello Frank.' Winne tried to lighten the mood by saying.'

'I thought the service was beautiful. Joanna and I couldn't get over how you spoke about the lads. It was unusual. I wish all funerals could be like that; it's more about the lads.'

'The way the church sees it, the wake is your opportunity to talk and remember the person. The mass is sacred. I'm not saying I'll get in trouble with the bishop, but they would frown on it becoming popular, making funerals too personal too casual.' The priest paused for a moment, then said

'Frank, I'm aware that you go back on active service in a few days.'

'It's about the letters, isn't Father.'

'Well, Frank, we have to make a decision. I think you know I'm against giving them to the family

'I want to give them to the families, but I can't let go of them.' Winnie sat next to him

'Come on; love, don't upset yourself.' The priest was determined, ignoring her, he urges him.

'Frank, the letters have become a burden to you; give them to me; I'll take responsibility for them.' Joanna asked.

'What will you do with them, Father.' He dismissed the question.

'I wouldn't concern yourselves with that I'll do the right thing with them.'

'And what's that?' Joanna's face was red with anger.

'Well, I'll destroy them.'

'Why? Frank interrupted her.

'Please, let's hear what the Father has to say.'

'There is nothing to be gained by giving them to the families apart from more heartache and pain.' Winnie, with her voice full of emotion, shouted.

'No, that's wrong.' Frank pattered her hand.

'Winnie, let him speak.'

'I perfectly understand how you feel, but you have to know how deep and painful the family grief is. There are eight hundred parishioners in this parish. I have to deal with all aspects of their pastoral care in the last week alone; I've had twenty burials. On

Wednesday, I gave a man the last rights while he was trapped under a staircase. Then I have to sit with each family and try and help guide them pray and with them. I never sleep night after night with people calling for my help.' Winnie spoke up.

'Father, we know what you do. Without you, this community would fall apart.'

'But you see, Frank, if you give them the letters, it's me who has to pick up the pieces they can't take anymore I can't take anymore, this would drive a stake through their hearts six letters, six broken families.'

'Don't you think the letters would help?' The priest looked at Joanna as she asked.

'No, it wouldn't; most of them are struggling with their faith, struggling to come to terms with what happened to them. They may turn away from the church and start to blame God. These letters would cause so much pain and damage it's not worth it.'

'So your saying destroys the letters and says no more, but we know about them.'

'In time, you'll understand why we have to take this decision together. We can share the burden. If you have doubts, I'm here to help you; believe me, it will get easier, and you'll know it's the right decision.' Winnie answered him.

'Don't you think it would get easier for the families? I think the letters would bring them comfort.'

'No, you're wrong; it won't, and it'll be on your conscious. You're lucky, Winnie; God gave you Frank back.' Frank gripped the arms of his chair with the veins in his neck visible, he shouted.

'Lucky, did you say lucky. It wasn't God who saved me; it was a clerk at the Admiralty. Someone tossed a coin in the air, and I came home when I should be at the bottom of the sea. I'm no more than a ghost. People look at me. I know what they're saying; Why him! Why him! Why was he spared? Sometimes I think I can hear the lads calling me. 'Come on, Frank, what are you doing there' I try to answer them and wake up screaming.' Winnie knelt beside him.

'Oh, love, come on, your home safe. Those lads would tell you; I know what they'd say get your backside off the chair and get back in the fight. Mogsy would say we're behind on points, but there are two rounds to go. Tommo would grab you by the scruff of your neck, and what did he always say 'empty glasses never got anyone drunk.' With tears in his eyes, he said.

'Why do I feel like I've let them down.'

'You haven't, my Frank; he'd never let them down; they all looked up to you. How many times did you get them out of trouble?' The priest suggested.

'Would it help if we prayed?'

'I don't think that will change things.'

'Winnie's right, Father. I need time to think. Thanks for coming. Joanna, please see Father out.' As he stood, he made one last attempt to convince him.

'I beg you. Frank destroy those letters.' Frank met his gaze, saying.

'Goodnight, Father.'

Two days before he was to go back on duty, Frank had placed everything on his bed.

'I think I've got everything.' Winnie sat down.

'What time did they say the boat sails'

'Second tide Saturday, so we've got plenty of time.' Winnie laughed, saying.

'I've put the Christmas tree back up, and you haven't opened your presents. I don't know how Joanna did it; that beef joint smells lovely.'

Joanna called from downstairs.

'I've just put the potatoes in. Shouldn't take long.'

Later as they sat eating, Frank asked.

'Where did you get the joint.' Smiling, Joanna said.

'Loose lips sink beef joints, so don't ask.' He looked at her with a smile.

'Let me guess, Bill, the friendly policeman. I wonder if he found the dog.' Pausing for a moment, he said, 'I've decided what I'm doing with the letters.'

'Oh! Frank, what's your decision.'

'Do you remember the other night when Father Maguire said six letters six broken families, well he was wrong; there was the seventh letter.' Joanna asked.

'A seventh one I don't understand.'

Frank took an envelope out of his pocket and handed it to Winnie.

'It's the seventh letter; please read it.' She gazed at the name on the front, looking at Joanna, she said.

'It's addressed to me, but I don't understand.' Ripping it open, she said. 'It's off you, Frank.' She attempted to read it. 'Dear . . .I Can't read it; Joanna, you do it.' Joanna looked at it for a moment, then read out loud.

'Well, Love things the same on our holidays. Don't sleep well as the lads are plagued with wind; no one will own up, ha-ha. Tell Joanna I've marked the whisky bottle, so tell her to keep it safe. I want to say how much I love you and say it keeps me together. I whisper I love you every day.

I wish I could hold you now. I'd never let you go. I haven't said this much, but Joanna is a beautiful friend to you and me. I'm glad we have her in our life. Well, love got to go looking after the lads is a full-time job in its self, ha-ha

Take care, my darling. See you soon

Frank

'Winnie, if I had gone down on the ship, would you have wanted the letter.' Sobbing, she said.

'Oh Frank, yes, I would keep it close to my heart forever.'

'I knew you would say that. Have we got any envelopes?'

'Yes, love in the draw.'

'I need six; help me with the names.' Frank walked out of the room.

'Frank, where are you going.'

'Get our coats and make this right.'

Joanna's flat.

Rita took a handkerchief out of her pocket and wiped her eyes.

'That was lovely, thank God he gave them the letters. I didn't like that priest. Did anyone ask why he didn't give them sooner?'

'On our way to the first house, I stopped them and told Frank to say he didn't know the lads had put them in his bag and he'd only just found them. The rest of that day was a blur. Full of tears, hugs and whisky. Frank said they squeezed him so hard his ribs cracked. We went back and had leftovers from Christmas dinner. The three of us fell asleep in front of the fire.'

'Please tell me Frank survived the war.'

'Yes, he did; he never got over the loss of all his mates, Winnie never left his side. The families would invite them to parties and weddings; I suppose they felt close to their loved ones having him there.' Rita stood up, looking at her watch; she said.

'I'll have to go, remember the doctor wants you to come to the surgery. I'll be here Wednesday morning. If you're not interested in the care home, I can apply for home help. Have to think about it.' Mai asked Joanna.

'When she born.'

'What date is your birthday?'

'Twentieth May Fifty Six, why do you ask.' Mai laughed, saying.

'My brother same month year of the horse.' Joanna smiled.

'Mai could tell you all the names of the new year; yours was the horse.'

Wednesday morning. Rita sat with lots of papers on her knee.

'I've spoken to the housing department; they say you are a priority for re-housing, and they have some new bungalows not far from here. Think about it no more broken lifts or stairs.' Joanna looked at the papers for a moment.

'That sounds lovely; leave them on the table, and I'll think about it.' Rita wanted to urge her to take up the offer but realised it would be better to let her take time. Joanna wanted to continue her story.

'When Frank went back on duty, Winnie and I did so much together, so you can imagine how she felt when I told her I was going to be a nurse. I'd seen a newspaper article about the shortage of nurses, so I applied; the interview was a formality, and then I'd do six weeks of training. I achieved the title of Auxiliary Nurse. Later, to my dismay, I became an expert in cleaning bedpans and then promoted to general dogsbody.' Rita asked.

'Were bombs still falling.'

'No, it had been months since the last ones; you can thank the RAF for that. One morning the matron asked to see me.'

Sefton Hospital Liverpool November 1943.

'We've had a request from the military asking for nurses to work in the south of England at an army hospital. They want nurses who don't have children, preferably single as you fit their criteria, would consider this.' Joanna thought for a moment, then answered.

'If I can develop and not just empty bedpans, then I would. I want to train as much as I can.' The matron agreed with her.

'The army nursing corps is a bit of an elite club, mainly from middle-class backgrounds. That's not to say they aren't good; I'm sure they're fine, but be aware that with the introduction of nurses from different parts of society, don't be surprised if they keep their distance. My advice is to keep your head down, say nothing and do your job.' Later, when she broke the news, Winnie's eyes filled up.

'When do you go.'

'In three days. Would you look after my house while I'm away?' Winnie hugged her, saying

'I'll polish and clean it every day.' Joanna laughed.

'Are you saying my house is untidy, although the sideboard is a bit dusty?'

'Promise me you'll come back.'

'Of course, I will.'

She had to wait three hours in Birmingham for the Edinburgh to London train; the platform was overcrowded with hundreds of sailors, soldiers and the odd blue uniform of the RAF. There was a mad scramble to get on when the train came in. A platform inspector rescued her, calling out.

'Now now, lads! this lady is expecting a baby; go easy.' Pushing them to one side, he winked at her as he helped her on the train, whispering he said.

'It works every time; you won't have a problem finding a seat.' Sadly, the last bit wasn't true; every carriage was full. She walked the whole length of the train. The last one had a couple passionately kissing. A man was obscured by a newspaper near the window; she could see the top of a bowler hat as he hid behind it. Sitting opposite him, she did her best to avoid looking at the couple. Joanna laughed to herself; Mai's voice came into her head 'they look for wasp.' The honeymoon couple suddenly stopped realising they had an audience and quickly left. The newspaper slowly dropped and revealed a Chinese man, impeccably dressed in a black dinner jacket and pinstriped trousers. She thought he looked in his late forties; large horn-rimmed glasses made his eyes look bigger. On his knee was a small leather briefcase. On the top of it etched into the leather was a pattern of a pair of glasses. He spoke first.

'I'm sorry you had to witness that, most inappropriate.' For a moment, a thought crossed her mind that China seemed to follow her. Without thinking, she replied in Chinese.

'It's no problem.' For a few moments, he sat frozen, only moving when his case fell on the floor. In shock, he replied in Chinese.

'You speak Chinese.'

'Yes, I lived in Shanghai for a few years.'

'I haven't spoken my language for five months. It's a relief to talk to you. I was staying in hospital accommodation and would talk to myself so that I wouldn't forget, people in the next room must have thought two people in the room with me.' Joanna hesitated before asking him.

'Have you been unwell?' Smiling, he replied.

'No, I've been studying to be an eye surgeon at the hospital in Edinburgh. I'm an optician, but this is my last chance to qualify. My shop is in London Soho. I was at Limehouse before that; fortunately, we had just moved when the bombs fell. I lost so many friends, all my customers, I don't think anyone survived.' He took a business card out of his pocket. It read Sammy Woo, Ophthalmologist, 15 Soho London.

'Thank you; if I need my eye testing, I'll call you.' Sammy sat next to her.

'I can't wait to get home. I have two daughters who I missed so much. My wife cooks the best meals; she'll have a banquet waiting for me. Now please tell me about you.'

'Well, how long have you got.'

Joanna talked about her journey from Liverpool and the beautiful places. She told him about Monique, and the first time she saw Shanghai. Joanna avoided talking about George and Mai.

'When I came back to Liverpool, I was a bit lost; like you, I needed to speak Chinese, so I ended up in Chinatown. I made so many friends there. I loved sitting in Zhang Whi café; we would talk for hours.' It was as if an electric shock had hit him; moving away from her, breathing heavily, he gasped.

'Did you say Zhang Whi?'

'Yes, do you know him?' Sammy jumped up and walked up and down.

'I know of him; there are many stories about Zhang Whi.' He sat opposite her, gazing at her for a few moments. In a whisper, he said.

'Are you The Shanghai Lady?' Joanna wanted to say no.

'Yes.' Sammy sat motionless after a while; Joanna asked him 'Are you alright?' Without speaking, he shook his head then sat back as if exhausted speaking softly, he said.

'I have heard so many stories about you. My daughters love the one where you fight a green snake. He would roam the world, killing people; then he would eat their souls. Their ghost would be lost, restless never to visit loved ones. Then he attacked the boat people on the bund. His prize was the soul of the river princess; this was so precious he didn't eat it but kept it in a leather bag around its neck. People pray every night for someone to help. The shanghai lady appeared as a golden kingfisher; she was so brave that she hunted the snake. The snake never knew fear; he promised to kill the kingfisher and put its body in his bag. They fought in the clouds for a hundred days, but the snake became slow, and the kingfisher pierced his heart with its long beak.' Joanna couldn't believe what she was hearing.

'I'm shocked. Do people think I'm a superwoman? I'm just ordinary.' Sammy sat forward and took both of his hands in his.

'You have given them hope. Your story has lit a flame that burns brighter than the sun. I know what you did and, for many people, a reason to fight, a reason to believe, children fall asleep to stories of the Shanghai Lady fighting dragons, killing mad emperors.' They hadn't noticed that the train had stopped; the board outside said Euston Station. On the far side of the station, Joanna could see a large group of women standing by a sign, 'nurses assembly point.' Sammy took his hat off and shook her hand.

'Please come to my shop, my wife will make us a meal, and you can meet my family.' Smiling, she said.

'That's a promise.'

Joanna's flat

'They thought you were a god; that's unbelievable.' Joanna replied.

'It's incredible to think I killed someone and became a saint. George died in a gutter naked full of opium and became a national hero. It doesn't make sense. When I hear these stories, they are about someone else, not me. I'm certainly not a god or a saint.' Rita asked.

'Did you go to Sammy's shop?'

'Yes, but not before I'd settled into the training college. We were given accommodation in an old boarding school, sleeping in dormitories with five other nurses. It took a bit of getting used to; there was little privacy, but I settled and made new friends. The girl next to me was an Irish girl Siobhan McMahon from Dublin, with the most beautiful accent; the only problem was she would say the most outrageous things. She often talked in Gaelic, constantly saying 'focail dheth' at the end of every sentence.' Rita asked.

'What did it mean?'

'No one ever asked her. I did one day, and she said it means fuck off. It started when she was about thirteen years old. She couldn't help it. When she went to confession, penance got longer and longer.' Laughing Rita said.

'Poor girl sounds like she had Tourette's. How was she accepted into the college?'

'Well, apart from the swearing, she was a gifted student, but she could drink. One Saturday night, on one of the rare occasions we were allowed out, she got drunk and started a fight with some Canadian soldiers, convinced they were Germans. I managed to get her away as some of the other nurses gave them first aid. She could throw a punch like a prize-fighter. Siobhan was a devout Catholic who wanted to go to mass. I couldn't understand this after the horrors and abuse she'd faced from the church. What kind of faith did she have? Way did she want to go? She said I had a calming influence on her and would go with her. The last time I went into a church was with Monique. I said yes, as it was an opportunity to light some candles. We sat in the back of a packed church; as the mass progressed, she gripped my hand tighter and tighter. I could see her biting her lip, forcing a 'focail dheth' back down her throat. She didn't take communion as it would have been disastrous. Then she let go as the congregation sang 'God Bless Our Pope.' None of them noticed Siobhan's 'Fuck Off' at the end of each verse.' Rita couldn't stop laughing.

'That's hilarious; she sounds a great character.' Joanna joined in the laughing.

'We were like two schoolgirls, giggling and laughing in bed, the other nurses complaining they couldn't sleep. She was wonderful. I wish Mai could have met her. We got different postings; both of us cried that day. She didn't say goodbye; she hugged me and said fuck off. I said you could fuck off as well. Siobhan fell on the bus screaming, laughing.'

'Our training was more than first aid; they gave us books on surgery with pictures of operations. We learned about surgical instruments and dealt with blast wounds and shrapnel wounds. There were rumours of something big about to happen.' Curious Rita said.

'What was that.'

'D, Day.'

Newland College London December 1943.
All the nurses assembled in the main hall as dignitaries walked onto the stage. In the middle of them was an army surgeon. He stood and addressed the meeting.

'Firstly, I'd like to thank all of you for signing up and answering the call of duty. Over the next few weeks, you'll be assigned to different hospitals in the south of England. We have an awards ceremony whenever we have a new intake of students, but these are exceptional times, so we'll have to dispense with the customary formalities. The good news is you have all qualified as Army Field Hospital Nurses.' The audience became animated with laughter and applause. 'I can't give you all a certificate today that will come sometime later, but what I can give you is three days off.' Their cheers could be heard all over London. As they were leaving the hall, Joanna was asked to go to a room in the college. Waking there, she racked her brains to see if's she'd done something wrong, as it felt she was in trouble. Three army officers sat behind a desk; in front of them were twelve nurses. Relieved she wasn't to be reprimanded, she sat down.

'I'm Major Pickford, and you must be wondering why you were summons here. All of you can speak different languages; put your hands up if you can speak German.' Four nurses put their hands up. 'Polish.' A few more did the same. 'French.' Six followed his request along with Joanna. 'There will be a need for you in the future with these skills. Not just looking after the wounded but civilian casualties as well. In the meantime, carry on with your duties and wait for further instructions.'

Joanna took advantage of her day off by going to visit Sammy. One of his daughters answered the phone; speaking in perfect English, she asked if she had an appointment; when Joanna said who it was, there was a long silence and then footsteps in the distance. Sammy spoke formally in Chinese.

'I'm delighted you called; my wife will prepare a meal.'

'Please don't go to too much trouble.'

Taking the Underground to Oxford Circus, she absorbed all the sights and sounds of a city at war. Everywhere you looked, men and women in uniform. Evidence of bombing is still visible in sandbags stacked up outside buildings. There had been no bombing for some time, thanks to the RAF. People still carry gas masks. The sounds of everyday life, people talking, laughing. In the distance, a church bell rang. Pausing standing still, she closed her eyes and lifted her head to the sun's warming rays. At that moment, she was back in her park in Liverpool on her way home and her mum's breakfast. On the corner of Soho Square and Frith St was Sammy's shop. Standing outside was Sammy guiding her inside; he spoke in Chinese.

'I haven't told anyone that you are here. There would have been a crowd. I'm not sure that would have been appropriate.'

The shop was pristine, with polished glass and dark oak desks, eye test boards and racks of spectacles on the walls. Climbing a flight of stairs at the shop's back, Joanna thought Mai's mother was standing at the top, next to their daughters. Sammy introduced her to his wife Chyou then guided her into his living room with a mixture of Chinese and English furniture. No one spoke for a few moments as they gazed at The Shanghai Lady. Joanna broke the silence holding her arms out to the girls, she said.

'Can I have a hug?' They nearly knocked her over as they embraced her. The youngest seven-year-old Ah Lam asked her.

'Is it true you have wings?' Ten-year-old Ling didn't say a word, just kept a tight hold of Joanna; it's not every day you hug a God. Joanna laughed as she explained.

'I don't have wings or do magic spells, well not today.' She winked at them. Sammy and his wife sat opposite on a sofa with the girls on either side.

'My wife has prepared some food, but first, I'd like to show you this.' Handing her an envelope. Inside was a letter confirming Doctor Sammy Woo has qualified as an ophthalmic surgeon.

'They want me to attend at a hospital in Eastbourne. It seems I'm in the army now.' Joanna congratulated him.

'That's fantastic news; your family must be so proud.' Chyou put her head down, saying.

'I've told him he mustn't fight; if he's in the army, they will give him a gun.' Smiling, Sammy reassured her.

'I keep telling you it's the medical army they don't fight.' Joanna thought for a moment then asked.

'Who will look after your business while your away.'

'I have an assistant who is quite capable; I'm in no doubt he'll do a great job while I'm away.'

The girls went to help their mother set the table as Sammy sat next to Joanna.

'Are you aware of the situation in Shanghai?' Joanna answered him.

'Yes, apart from the newspapers, I also speak to Zhang Whi every week.' Sammy looked worried as he spoke.

'Chyou has a brother in one of the prisons. There is talk of atrocities, starvation, and beatings every day. She wants me to ask you if she could have a lock of your hair. She believes if she sends it to him, he'll survive.' Thinking for a few moments, Joanna looked at him.

'The image they have of me is a fantasy. All these magical stories have grown because I killed a man. I could never live up to this woman; The Shanghai Lady has become folk law. It frightens me.'

'I understand how you feel; it is an incredible thing that has grown, but the ripples you created have turned into a tidal wave of hope. You fought and destroyed a demon; if you hadn't, then we wouldn't be having this conversation. Your bravery tells the people don't give up; it gives them courage a reason to fight.' Joanna hadn't had this conversation with anyone; now, the floodgates of emotion burst. From deep inside, she was overwhelmed.' Sammy looked at his wife in the kitchen and signalled her to close the door as she wept.

'I've tried to reconcile myself to what happened, but I have to keep my love for Mai in place, holding her in my arms, those final moments are frozen in my mind, I thought I'd grieved for her, but I haven't; now I have the burden of a God terrifies me. I'm so sorry; I've embarrassed you in front of your family.' Sammy thought for a moment.

'This Mai you talk about is the one thing that keeps you going forward. What would she say If she was here,' Joanna smiled through the tears?

'Oh! she would have said a saying her mother told her; it makes some sense and would have something to do with a chicken, river spirit or spice and soup.' Sammy took her hands, looking deep into her eyes.

'I think grieving for her would be difficult; she guides you; she hasn't left you. How often does she talk to you?'

'All the time.'

Although that food was in short supply, Chyou produced six courses. The girls couldn't take their eyes off her; Sammy told them off for staring. Joanna spoke.

'Sammy told me about your brother; I'd like to give you a lock of my hair. I could do with a haircut anyway, according to matron; it's too long.' Looking across the table, Sammy mouthed the words in English, 'thank you.' He reassured Joanna that his wife was good at cutting hair; she always did the girls, and when he sat still long enough, she cut his. It didn't take long for a large amount of hair to build up in the middle of the table. Joanna laughed, saying.

'There is enough for an army.'

Ghyou and the girls started rolling clumps into ring sized small braids wrapped with cotton. Joanna admired this little cottage industry and marvelled at how skilful they were; she even attempted to make a few herself, making the girls laugh as she fumbled her's. When they finished, Sammy counted them sixty in all. Joanna took a few for herself. They sat quietly for a few moments gazing at their work when Chyou said a prayer.

'Take the breath of the new day and fill each strand; let its power grow wings and carry you home.'

As they said their goodbyes, Cyhou clung to Joanna both of them cried. The girls took their turns to hug her and kiss her. Sammy took hold of her hands, saying.

'Many birds sing in the mountains so far away, yet their song is in your heart beating in time with the Kingfisher.' They embraced for a moment. 'Take care; we may see each other soon.'

She sat on the tube train, tired and yet at peace. She imagined sitting on her bed telling Mai all about Sammy and his family. At one of the stations, a woman asked her whether the seat next to her was taken. Without thinking, she replied in Chinese.

'Yes, please sit down.' Surprised at her answer, the woman walked away. Later in her room, Joanna wrote a letter to Winnie; before she sealed it, she placed one of the rings inside, saying this is for Frank. She put Monique's last address and another ring on the second envelope.

Joanna's flat

Looking out of her window, she could see Rita parking her car. The lifts were still broken; it took time before she arrived at Joanna's door.

'I've had another phone call from your doctor. He said he looked through the letterbox and could see you; why didn't you open the door.'

'I thought it was one of those people canvassing for the election, although I might vote for the Monster Raving Lunatic Party, he was dressed as a sprout. A lovely young man he was hoping to be an architect; his girlfriend wouldn't walk up the stairs; she was dressed a carrot.' Rita went into the kitchen and prepared a meal as Joanna continued her conversation.

'My priority for anyone in the election would be to fix the lifts. Oh! I've just remembered I found a photograph the other day.' Rita carried a plate of sandwiches in and sat down. Joanna gave her the photograph. 'It was taken at the field hospital in Portsmouth. Look at all those tents, the one I'm standing outside was my new home.' Rita surveyed the image of five nurses, all linking arms.

'Is that you on the right.'

'Yes, and the girl next to me is Siobhan. She did go to another hospital but got transferred to mine after some misdemeanour. It seems a porter got too close, so she punched him, attending to his first aid needs when he regained consciousness.'

Field Hospital Portsmouth January 1944.

Joanna and Siobhan were sent to the Surgical tent and gown up. The sister in charge informed them there had been an accident some soldiers were injured during a training exercise; she used the word 'a sympathetic discharge.' Confused, they looked at her; it seemed a grenade went off when it shouldn't. He was in

his early twenties; the left side of his body was pitted with minor wounds. The surgeon spoke in a clipped English accent.
'This won't be the first type of injuries you'll encounter. The fragments close to the surface will need to be extracted, taking great care to minimize further tissue damage to the surrounding areas. Pieces that have penetrated deeper may well have to be left, the extent of which will only be visible by x-ray.' Standing back, he observed them. As Joanna went through her examination, checking his level of consciousness, examining his eyes and ears, she could hear the surgeon saying, 'good.' For a moment, she was back in Shanghai. Kneeling by the burnt-out army wagon, dead soldiers lying twisted on the ground. Looking down at Mai, she was in her arms smiling, saying, 'it's ok' The few bits of shrapnel in her leg began to ache, her head spinning; she wanted to run out and scream. Before the horror of what happened overwhelmed her, a moment of comedy came to her rescue. Siobhan gently rolled him on his side; he moaned for a moment but stopped as the morphine relieved his pain. From his neck to the top of his leg had extensive wounds.'
'Fucking hell.' Siobhan said loudly. The surgeon replied.
'My sentiments entirely, although you can't put that in his medical notes.' Was it shock or Tourette's that made her say it? It seemed to wake Joanna up. For the next hour, they worked together, and the clink of bits of metal hitting a bowl grew. Siobhan displayed great skill in removing each piece fast, all the time the surgeon repeated 'Good, good.' When they had finished, the soldier was taken out. Joanna was exhausted, breathing heavily as the surgeon said,
'I must say that you two work well as a team. Your attention to detail was first class. If we receive an injury requiring amputation, I'll call you to observe. You won't be doing one but supporting a surgeon is vital. In the months ahead, you'll need as much experience as you can get. Under normal circumstances, you would not take the role of a doctor, but whatever lays ahead, we must be ready. If we are overrun with casualties and a doctor may not be available, so you'll do your best. We have to save lives. This would only be in the most extreme circumstances.'

Sitting on her bed, Joanna poured her heart out, telling her about Mai and Shanghai. Siobhan listened and then said.

'I can imagine what that must have felt like to lose the one true love in your life. Ting is I lost my wee baby in the few moments I had with her. I'd never known such joy. They took her from me then put me in prison fuck off; well, it was a workhouse for the devil brides.' Joanna, shocked, asked.

'How could they do that? What about the father.'

'Ting is I had six brothers; it was anyone of them. They wouldn't listen to me, saying I encouraged them. My saying fuck off all the time was the devil talking.'

'How old were you.'

'I was thirteen. I was kept in a cell for three years because I would contaminate the other girls. Then my chance came when they moved me to another prison. Two priests took me into a room and scrubbed my mouth out with soap fuck off. A piece got stuck in my throat, and I'd stopped breathing. Waking up in a hospital, I thought I'd died and was in haven. A nun sat outside in case the devil came to rescue me. He didn't turn up, but an open window did. The nurse's home was opposite. I picked the nicest clothes and shoes. I climbed on a bicycle and went like the wind fuck off.'

'How did you come to England.'

'That was the easy bit. I just walked onto a boat bound for Liverpool. Fortunately, the young lad on deck pulling the rope up smiled at me. I smiled back. I told him I was on the run from the Pope, fuck off, his family were all in the Orange Lodge, only too happy to help. I stayed with his aunty; she was ancient, so I did everything for her. After that, I did many jobs and emptied bedpans in a hospital fuck off. They seemed to like me as the sisters on different wards would ask for me. Now I'm here with you.'

In the next few days, rumours spread about the big push. They spent more time in the surgical tent. One morning, they were summoned to a meeting with the major who recruited them for their language skills.

'I only speak Gaelic; do French people speak it?' Siobhan whispered as they sat in a meeting room. Joanna looked around and counted the nurses.

'Twenty-six, that's not a lot. I wonder what he wants.' She could see a clipboard being passed around. An officer was giving instructions on what to write.

'Put your name, tent number and language you speak.' Joanna could see Siobhan was becoming nervous and animated. The officer was only interested in one of the nurses as he made conversation with her. Joanna wrote next to Siobhan's language, 'Gallic.'

'What does that mean.' Siobhan was confused. Joanna whispered.

'It sounds the same as Gaelic; Gallic means French, so if they ask, it can be a simple error, a misunderstanding a mistake.' Siobhan smiled as she replied.

'They have a saying in Liverpool if you get caught, just act fucking soft.' Some of the nurses looked around to see who was giggling. The major entered and stood at the front.

'I've asked all of you here today and explain why you have attended operations in the surgical tent. If and when the big push happens, we will establish forward emergency field hospitals. These hospitals will be close to the battle lines. It's likely the situation will be very fluid and fast-moving. The thinking about this is speed, assessing casualties, stabilising, and then evacuating the wounded to rear hospitals. Listen to the army medics to have information vital to the patient's survival. You will be supporting army surgeons, but because you are so close to the theatre of war, the experience you have gained will be used only as a last resort. Your language skills will be vital as you do your assessments if they don't speak English. You are likely to see civilians and enemy soldiers. You'll all be given small diaries; any information you receive must be recorded and passed on. This information could be of great military importance to the war effort. You'll have a badge signifying the language you can speak. Any questions.'

A nurse asked.

'When is this likely to happen?' The major laughed as he answered.

'I'm sure Hitler would like to know. Everyone has been using the phrase 'The Big Push.' Which sounds like a baby is about to be born; the short answer is we don't know; we have to be ready.'

Joanna's flat

'That was January nineteen forty-four. We didn't set foot in France until December. Back at the camp, most of the casualties were minor injuries caused by boredom, football, and fights; we were asked to go to the maternity hospital one day. I'd seen Mai's sister being born; this was wonderful, an escape from the constant training. I wasn't sure if it was a good idea for Siobhan to be there; she wept, holding the first one. There's was no way of telling the staff her story.'

Rita had been knocking for some time before Joanna opened the door.

'I was beginning to think you'd gone out.' Joanna gave a confusing answer.

'I thought you were in the kitchen.'

'You go and sit down. I'll make you something to eat.' Joanna continued her conversation.

'Before we were posted to France, I was given ten days' leave. It was a joy to be back home. Winnie was fine she'd had letters from Frank, saying the weather was sweltering where he was; this was a coded message because he would be somewhere cold, probably on a convoy to Russia. The first two days, I slept under the sideboard; I did have a lot to tell Mia.' Mai sat up and laughed.

'She talks so much she couldn't blow a candle out.'

'Mai would say if it was my birthday, I couldn't blow candles out talking so much. I was able to visit Chinatown. Sadly, the news from Shanghai wasn't good. Zhang Whi told me they have started rounding up anyone the Japanese consider a threat without evidence or trial. More stories of brutality. I gave him six hair rings Sammy's daughters made.' Rita asked.

'When did you go to France.'

'Tenth of December nineteen forty-four. When we got off the ship, we had to walk half a mile in a snowstorm.'

Tenth December 1944 Franch.
Joanna and Siobhan couldn't believe their luck as they walked frozen and wet into a Chateau. It had been the command headquarters for the Allies—ten bedrooms hot and cold running water with central heating. As the head nurse assigned them their rooms, she informed them they would be shared with five other nurses. That didn't matter; it wasn't a tent. After an evening meal, a medical liaison officer led a meeting in what would have been a small ballroom.

'In two days, you'll be travelling to a field hospital in Belgium. There will likely be many casualties. This is what you have trained for.; you've all demonstrated excellent teamwork, and we are in no doubt that you all will carry out your duties with distinction. In the meantime, get as much rest as you can. Walking back to their bedrooms, no one spoke. Joanna recognised some of the nurses from the college. One of them produced two bottles of brandy. The mood lightened as they sat on their beds. Laughter echoed as a tipsy Siobhan broke the world record in 'fucks' followed by the filthiest jokes. On a cold Wednesday morning, they set off. Sitting in the back of an army wagon, they looked out at a flat landscape. A convoy of vehicles occasionally skidded behind them as the frost had hardened the ground. Eventually, they arrived at the Field hospital, which was identical to all the others, only this one had wooden walkways through a warren of tents. Thankfully their tent had a wood burner in the middle and had thick blankets on the beds. Warming their hands, Siobhan said.

'How long do you tink we'll be here?'
'If we knew that, we could book a holiday. Let's hope it's not too long.'
A liaison officer came in and told them to go to the theatre tent.
'Casualties have started to arrive.'
The first two soldiers survived a few minutes; nothing could be done, their injuries extensive. Five hours had passed before Joanna and Siobhan had a break; the surgeon thanked them.

Covered in blood, they left. Outside, ambulances queued up with more wounded. Once they had changed, they were directed to the minor injured tent. An American soldier lay on his stomach. His bottom was peppered in shrapnel. Opposite him, another soldier, his trousers torn, his legs bleeding. The one laying down said.

'You don't mind if I don't get up.' The second one laughed, saying.

'Looking at your arse, it's an improvement on your face.'

'Yeah, well, you shouldn't be looking; that's the job of the generals twenty miles away puffing on their cigars.' The two comrades traded jokes while Joanna and Siobhan began cleaning them up. Two more nurses came in to concentrate on the one lying down.

'When you girls finish tiding us up. How do you fancy a few beers.' The Sargent stood in the doorway for a few moments before he spoke.

'How are you guy's doing.' One of them answered.

'We are doing great, two nurses each; that's always been my fantasy. How's Mitch and Collins? They got their own nurses.' The Sargent paused for a few moments before saying.

'They didn't make it.' The one laying down replied.

'That's a shame Collins owed me twenty bucks.' The other soldier put his head down and wept.

The casualties became fewer as the fighting stopped at the end of January. Some of the nurses said that the Germans were starting to retreat. Joanna and Siobhan had a week off where they slept most days. No matter how experienced they were, nurses could be heard crying in their sleep. The next few weeks saw more civilian casualties as they fled the war. Instead of bullet wounds, they now treated blistered feet, dysentery and exhaustion.

Joanna's flat Liverpool 1981.

'You haven't been taking your tablets.' Rita had the box in her hand.

'Oh, I don't need them every day; they don't work.'

'The tablets are for a reason. You know that you were a nurse yourself.' Rita did her best not to get angry, but Joanna had her answer.

'Will the tablets stop me from getting older? That's the one thing the Americans did in the war; they could supply you with everything they might have had tablets for eternal youth. We had that many bedpans; the nurses used them as plant pots. I'd lost count of the days and months; we were about forty miles from Paris in early August. There were a few days when no casualties came, so Siobhan and I walked into a local village. It was as if the war had ended as we walked up a small high street; we could see chairs and tables outside a café.

Saint-Germain-en Laye Aurgust 1945
Joanna ordered drinks. Siobhan laughed at Joanna's speaking French.
'I can't get used to it; you become a different woman.'
'I must sound like Monique. She taught me to copy what she said; that's her voice you can hear.' Siobhan smiled as she spoke.
'I went to that soldier, remember the one who cried.' Surprised, Joanna asked.
'Why?'
'Ting is, when he cried, I knew that sorrow reached out to me. You don't think I'm mad, do you, all the men I've ever known have hurt me fuck off. This solider, I don't understand why I wanted to help. The ting is I got in a load of trouble fuck off. I went to see him sit by his bed; we talked. Oh, he has a lovely smile, and told me all about his family in Oklahoma; he has two sisters who live on a farm. His parents are farmers with two hundred cattle. Then the charge nurse came over and asked me to step outside fuck off. She gave me a proper old telling off. You shouldn't be in this ward; fraternising with the patient is strictly forbidden fuck off. She chased me from the out. I'll let you off this time, she said, because your Irish and don't understand the rules.'
'What are you going to do.'
'He told me they are shipping him back home on Friday. I went back not to the tent. I went around the back and cut a small hole in the canvas next to his bed so we could talk fuck off. The other nurses must have felt sorry as he looked like he was talking

to himself. He gave me his address and wanted me to write to him. I hope you don't mind. I've given him your address.'

'What about the people you live with? Couldn't he write there?' Siobhan shook her head.

'God no, they're all nutters fuck off. Anyway, I've put my name down to travel with the injured soldiers on Friday so I can see him off and say goodbye.'

'Sounds serious.'

'That's it; what does love feel like how do you know what it is. You told me about Mai; how did you feel when you knew you loved her.' Joanna was back in her bedroom dancing with Mai. With tears in her eyes, she said.

'I felt every part of me was reborn; I couldn't breathe holding onto her. I never wanted to let her go. The whole world made sense because of her. Every moment was incredible; she made me complete.' Siobhan thought for a moment.

'Fucking hell is that what I've got to look forward to. It's a knot in my stomach at the moment. When I close my eyes, I can see his smile. Is that right?'

'Well, it's a start. As you're saying goodbye to your boyfriend, I'm going to Paris.'

A group of nurses arranged a truck to take them into Paris, the back of which was open; fortunately, the weather was perfect. Singing and laughing, they made their way occasionally; American jeeps would overtake them, Soldiers, holding up bottles of wine shouting 'meet us by the Eifel Tower.' Crossing the Seine, Joanna noticed the buildings were tall, elegant balconies with wrought iron railings. Large windows open, and people are standing, some sitting as if they were waiting for a parade to pass by. The driver stopped by the Arc de Triomphe and informed them they had to be back at six sharp. Joanna had seen pictures of the Champs-Elysees many times; she marvelled at how wide the boulevard was; before her was a sea of celebration, hundreds of men, women and children crowding the pavements. Soldiers in all kinds of vehicles drive up and down, beeping their horns. One driver had a girl sitting on his lap pouring wine into his mouth. Opening her purse, she took out one of Monique's business cards; the address was 'Rue Faubourg

-Saint-Honore' thankfully, there was a small map with directions on the back. It took her half an hour to find it standing at the top of the road; she gazed at pavement cafés full of people drinking. In the distance, groups of people carrying buckets of bricks and masonry tipped them onto a mound. As she approached, it was a shop destroyed by fire. The yellow Star of David is painted on the wall on either side of the front, although blackened by smoke still visible. Checking the card, this was Monique's shop.

'Have you come to gloat.' A woman in her thirties covered in dust approached her. For a moment, Joanna thought she would hit her with a spade. Stepping backwards, Joanna said.

'I'm sorry, I don't know what you mean.'

'The Germans painted the sign, but French people set fire to it. What do you want?'

'Well, firstly, I'm English, and the woman who owned the shop was my friend Monique Wiseman. I'm trying to find any news about her.' A man in his seventies ended the confrontation; his black suit was also covered in dust.

'Please forgive my daughter for some people watching our destruction has become a hobby. I'm Samuel Stine; how do you know Monique?'

'My name is Joanna Barlow. I travelled with her a few years ago to China. We became friends she did write to me for some time, the last letter she was in Vienna. I've heard nothing since.'

'I have an apartment just around the corner. Would you be my guest? I'm sure my wife would like to speak to you, also I need to change my clothes.'

She gazed up; the building was classical; the entrance had floors and walls of light marble in stark contrast to the devastation in Monique's shop. The wrought Iron lift is clean and polished with an oak panel supporting a gilt-edged mirror. Joanna guessed that they had money. The corridor was wide with large rosewood doors; Ruth, his wife, stood and welcomed her. Samuel spoke in Yiddish. Then he introduced her in French. Ruth asked.

'Have you heard from Monique? We've been so worried.'

'Not for some time.'

The front room was large, with tall windows. There were no pictures or ornaments, just a table and four chairs. In the corner were two makeshift beds on the floor. Samuel informed her.

'I'm afraid the apartment is poorly furnished. The Germans came looking for us, disappointed at not finding anyone, they helped themselves to everything. When they invaded, we went into hiding; two weeks ago, was the first time we looked at the sky in years. The Wisemans were friends of ours.' Joanna asked.

'Were you in the jewellery trade?'

'No, I was in Shipping Import and Export, trans-Atlantic. I knew her family from the synagogue. You met my daughter before; well, Monique would babysit for us.' Ruth had a book of photographs and began pointing to ones with Monique on. Joanna was fascinated looking into her past. Pictures in and around Paris, some were sitting in a park with children next to her. One with a younger Samual, Ruth and another man.

'That's Monique's uncle; he had a heart attack two weeks after this photograph; when she lost Peter, she would always be available to mind children it helped her with her grief. I think she would have been a wonderful mother. By then, her family had disowned her. I told Samual that I would embrace her if it were my daughter.'

Joanna smiled as she looked at this handsome couple. There is a photograph of Peter and Monique sitting on a bench, the Eiffel Tower in the distance. It reminded her of the photo of her and Mai on their big adventure sitting in The Metropole Hotel. Running her fingers across the image, she felt closer to her. Ruth continued her commentary of the album.

'Peter was a wonderful man they were so much in love. I told her family they were wrong; they never spoke to us for years. We can't reconcile; they were all taken to the east on a cattle train. I pray every day that they survived. Her life became the business we didn't see much of her as she travelled the world.' She pointed to a large family photo. 'That was at her sister's wedding; you can see her mother and father on either side of the happy couple. There are twenty people on it, all taken to the death camps. Monique would have been on that if she hadn't met Peter'.

Samual asked Joanna why she was in Paris.

'I'm in the Army Nursing Corps. It was my day off, and as I had one of her business cards, I wanted to find information or any news.'

'Even though we have no news, I feel that our friendship with her has drawn us closer. I'll give you, my address; we must keep in touch.' Joanna looked at her watch.

'I'm afraid I'll have to go. I want to light a candle at Notre Dame. Thank you so much.'

As she was leaving, Ruth gave her a copy of Monique and Peters photo. Later, Joanna sat looking at the two candles she lit near the altar while she held the image of the two lovers. The cathedral was packed, behind her, the steady drone of people saying the rosary. Closing her eyes, she could see Mai lying next to her, moonlight shining through the bedroom window. Tired, she made her way back to the Arc de Triomphe. Paris is still in party mode pavement cafés are overcrowded the smell of cognac and cigars everywhere. On the edge of a boulevard, she could see a café with lots of British personal sitting outside. In a corner, an army officer sat alone. Walking closer, she recognised him.

'Captain Crawford.' The look of surprise on his face made him jump up, knocking his drink across the table, rescuing it before it spilt its contents.

'Good God almighty Mrs Barlow, I can't believe it's you. Why are you in Paris? Please sit down. Can I get you a drink?' Joanna speaking French, ordered a glass of wine.

'I'm a nurse in the army nursing corps. It's my day off, so I wanted to see the city.'

'The nursing corps, who would have imagined that.'

'Well, we all have to do our duty for King and Country.' There was an element of sarcasm in her voice.

'You would have been close to the fighting. I can't imagine how difficult it must have been, the horrors you must have witnessed.' Looking directly at him, she said.

'We did our best for them. Can I ask you a question?' He leaned forward.

'Yes, by all means.'

'Did you know what George was doing?'

'I don't understand what you mean.'
'Well, you did say if he had business with Autile he was in danger.'
'I had heard about Autile, and It wasn't good.' Joanna smiled as she could see he was uncomfortable.
'Let me rephrase the question, what do you think he was doing.' He didn't answer and had the look of a man trapped.
'I don't know what you want me to say.'
'George was a pimp for Autile. They supplied a service to diplomats, government officials and the military.' He became angry, keeping his voice low, he said.
'That was the far east what we consider wrong in the home counties was the norm in Shanghai. Even in Roman times, they had brothels. Look where we are now. Paris had a reputation for some of the best brothels. Even the King of England would bathe in champagne with two prostitutes.'
'Were you aware that children as young as five procured for their entertainment? Autile told me George had an insatiable appetite for them.'
'You spoke to Autile.'
'Yes, but I'll come back to him. If you knew about these excesses, a word that seems to excuse them, did you do anything about it?' He gave a wry smile, answering.
'It would have been suicide to go against the establishment.'
'So, there was no one you could talk to, just turn a blind eye.'
'I worked my socks off to get where I am. I have a family; there wasn't anything I could do.' Joanna sipped on her drink and then said.
'Did you know about 'The Pot' the prize at the poker tournament?' Shaking his head, he looked at his watch. 'Well, I was the prize cherry-picked by George. A young white virgin coerced into a marriage highly prized in his circle of decadence. Do you remember the night the Japanese bombed the nightclub? I was to be delivered to the winner; Autile arranged a gold-plated bed as the grand finale. The losers watched the winner enjoying his trophy as I was raped. Autile said that I would join his staff entertaining the Japanese military; he said they would pay well

for an English woman. Three bombs spoiled his plans.' The captain became curious, asking.

'When did this conversation with Autile take place.' Looking straight at him, she said.

'Just before I killed him. You see, he wanted compensation for his loss of income, so he came to the house. Before trying to rape me, he politely explained his new opportunities with the Japanese. He gave me graphic details of the British establishment's thirst for all the delights his brothels could offer. Then he attacked me. He didn't see Mai come into the bedroom; she struck him with a metal ornament. I did the rest with one blow; his skull broke. After that, we placed him in his car and took the handbrake off, pushing him downhill.' Open-mouthed, he struggled to speak.

'Why are you telling me this.'

'You need to know the truth, the 'Do Nothings' people like you who live in your little world that always looks the other way. I've one last thing to tell you. I know who killed George, and it wasn't Autile, goodbye.'

As she met the other nurses, one of them asked her why she was smiling; her answer was.

'I've just met an old acquaintance.'

Joanna's flat

'Weren't you worried he'd report you?' Rita is engrossed in the story.

'Who would he tell? Even if he did, the establishment would promote him and sweep it under the carpet. Our time had come to an end in France. They gave us little diaries to record; the information we learned from civilians or enemy soldiers we treated. It was then to be passed to military intelligence. None of the nurses did instead of using them as personal diaries. Every night, I would write telling Mai what happened that day and how much I loved her. Looking back, I can't believe what we did. Sometimes we were so close to the fighting tents that would collapse from the blast of shells. Just when we thought the war was coming to an end, it threw us its parting shot.

'Everything was being packed up and shipped back. The French received ample medical supplies to help them with shortages, although we heard that some Americans had set up a black market mainly for cigarettes and whiskey. A few days before we left, Siobhan and I were in a first aid tent on the outskirts of a local town, mainly with minor injuries, a mixture of local people, women and children. From outside the tent, we could hear a commotion. They were shouting. 'tuer la chienne allemande'. Rita asked what did that mean. Joanna replied.

'Oh, sorry, it means to kill the German bitch. I couldn't believe it when the American soldiers brought her in. She was seventeen; Standing in her underwear, badly beaten, her head shaved, cuts and bruises all over her. To make matters worse, she was six months pregnant. A Sargent followed them.

France 1945

'They were about to kill her. Does anyone speak French?' Joanna said yes. 'Well, mam, there's a lynch mob half of them armed French resistance the Maquis. I'm not sure we can hold them off.' The noise outside grew louder, shouting.

'arracher le cancer allemande deleur ventre.' The Sargent asked what they were shouting as Siobhan cleaned the girl's injuries.

'Rip German cancer out of her belly.' Joanna translated.

'Christ, we might have to let her go.'

'I'll go out and talk to them.' Joanna volunteered; rubbing his chin, he said.

'It might buy us some time; we could hand her over to the Red Cross.'

Stepping outside, she was shocked at the size of the crowd. At least five men stood in front of her armed. The leader in a white shirt tall with a bony face remaindered her of Autile. Speaking in French, she addressed the mob.

'Liberated from a bunch of animals, and now you have turned into animals.' Someone called out sarcastically.

'Give her back; we'll look after her.'

'You've not done a good job up to now, have you—the nurses in these tents work to save lives. When the wounded are brought in, we don't ask who they are; we fight to save a life no more, no less. Killing this young girl and her baby might make you feel good for a brief moment, then what?' The bony faced leader lifted his gun and pointed it at Joanna's head. Without flinching, Joanna walked forward, so the barrel was touching her head. She thought she would be with Mai with a smile on her face if he pulled the trigger. Speaking softly, she said.

'I've heard you a poor shot, so I'll make it easy for you.' The crowd was in silence.

With her eyes closed, she could see Mai smiling. The watching audience must have wondered why she was taking a suicidal risk. Had they known her story, they would have applauded her bravery. Waiting for him to pull the trigger, she was at peace, ready to be with her love. The silence made her open her eyes in time to see him lower his gun, looking around; there were only a few people left. The rest of the gunmen were waiting for their leader to do something. Spitting on the ground in front of her, he turned and walked away. Joanna struggled to breathe. When she did sobbing and gasping, she almost fell.

'Would you consider joining the United States Army?' The Sargent asked. She gave a breathless reply

'I've had enough of war.'

'If you change your mind, call me at the command centre and ask for Sargent Doyle.

There was no sign of the girl and Siobhan back into the tent. The Sargent told her they had gone out the back. Running between the tents, she could see Siobhan sitting in the driver's seat of a staff car. Siobhan called to her.

'You took your fucking time.' In a panic, Joanna called out.

'Where's the girl.'

'Under a blanket in the back.'

'I didn't know you could drive?'

'My family in Liverpool taught me. Lots of stuff falls off the back of wagons, so we have to be sharp.' Joanna looked at her, saying.

'So, you are a getaway driver.' Siobhan answered with a grin.

'I'm saying nothing.'

At the nurses' compound, word had gotten out about Joanna and the girl. As they smuggled her in, the charge nurse waited for them, a serious woman who demanded the highest standards. With her clarion call, cleanliness and punctuality Gloria Joy was best known as the matron. She was neither Glorious nor Joyful; Joanna swallowed hard as she was about to be admonished; instead, she said.

'Well, you two seemed to have had an adventure. Does this girl have a name?' Quickly Joanna asked her.

'de quoi t'appelles-tu.'

'Yvette.'

The charge nurse organised two nurses to take Yevette for a bath. Turning to the rest of the nurses, she asked them to put a wardrobe together.

'Under normal circumstances, I would have dismissed you and your Irish cohort on the spot. But from what I've heard, you very nearly paid the ultimate sacrifice. There is no need for discipline.' Joanna said.

'I wouldn't let them take her.' The charge nurse face softened as she said.

'I don't know whether to hit you with a bedpan or give you the Victoria Cross; what the hell were you thinking.' Looking at Yevette, she asked. 'Does she have a family? We'll be gone in two days.' Turning to Yevette, Joanna asked.

'as-tu de la famille.'

'Bayeux Normandy j'ai une tante.' Joanna translated.

'Well, then we have to get her out to her aunt as soon as possible.'

Washed and cleaned, Yevette sat on a bed and told them how set met William, a German soldier. he was nineteen. They just fell in love; then the world turned upside down; she didn't even have time to say goodbye or even tell him she was pregnant as the German army abandoned Paris. Later Joanna and Siobhan sat watching Yevette sleeping. Siobhan asked.

'Were you frightened when he put the gun to your head?'

'No, I would have been with Mai. It wasn't until he walked away that it hit me.'

'Promise you won't do that again without saying goodbye.' Siobhan had tears in her eyes as she said it.

The next afternoon Sargent Doyle stood next to a truck as Yevette climbed into the front. All the nurses gathered to wave her off. Turning to Joanna, he said.

'I thought you changed your mind about joining the army when you rang.'

'Sorry to disappoint you, but you did say if I needed anything.' Banging the side of the truck was the signal for them to go, he replied.

'My guys will see she gets there.'

Joanna's Flat

'I can't believe you did that; he could have blown your brains out.' Rita said, shocked at Joanna's story.

'I've often thought about that moment. All I could see was Mai's face. I just wanted to be with her at that moment. Looking back, I can still feel the wind blowing and its rattling noise on the canvas tents. In the distance, the noise of heavy vehicles. I don't think he would have pulled the trigger, not with American troops watching. There were terrible reprisals against anyone who helped the Germans.' Standing at the back of a boat, Siodhan and I watched the coast of France disappear; we stood there in silence, so many memories.' Joanna paused for a moment, then said.

'Winnie must have polished the sideboard every day; Frank was demobbed from the navy. He got a job on the Mersey Ferries keeping the engines running smoothly; being on the water kept him close to the lads. The first few days, I slept under the sideboard. I would read the diary to Mai.'

'What about Siobhan? What happened to her.'

'I did receive letters from her soldier; Siobhan would call on a Sunday, and I made sure I had a roast on the go. Winnie got on excellent with her, although Frank did get annoyed as Winnie started saying fuck off a lot. Then she knocked on my door one morning with tickets in her hands; she was going to be with her soldier. The ship was sailing the next day to New York. The two of us cried and cried before she boarded it. Her last words to me were, I'm not going to tell you to fuck off; we tried to laugh but couldn't. Watching the ship leave, I was determined to return to China.'

'Did you go?'

'No, the whole country was in a terrible state. Eventually, The Cultural Revolution and a leader called Mao Tse-tung took over; it would have been impossible. I did my weekly visits to Chinatown to keep myself sane. One day I saw an advert in the paper for 'French Lessons at good rates, students' half-price.' I made contact; he was a retired school teacher; he gave me all the information I needed, so I set up on my own, advertised in the local newspaper started providing lessons. I didn't do too much academically, more conversational. I didn't need the money, but it was an excellent opportunity to talk to people. A steady stream of students came through the door; it was therapeutical for me; I met some lovely people. Then the city council did what the Luftwaffe couldn't do to demolish the house; they called it 'slum clearance'. There was nothing wrong with the house; the damage from the blitz had been repaired years before that didn't stop them; I ended up in this high-rise concrete block.'

'I've been meaning to ask you what happened to Sammy, the optician.'

'He did write to me his family were all well, the business had expanded to three shops. He was an eye surgeon now at the local hospital after spending most of his war at a military hospital in Kent. Word got out that he was a friend of The Shanghai Lady; not surprisingly, his company was given a boost, mainly amongst the Chinese community. His wife's brother came out of prison carrying the small hair ring Sammy's daughters had made; he did say many copies claiming to come from The Shanghai Lady had been made; I would be bald if I had provided more. Sometimes I dream of Mai and myself with The Shanghai Lady. She's so powerful and brave I would love to meet her. I see her as an older sister. Looking back over my life, I'm lucky to have known such strong women, Monique, Siobhan and Mai; to me, they are The Shanghai Ladies.'

Thursday morning.

'I've put the shopping away; you've got enough for a week. One of my colleagues will call in my place. Don't forget the doctor will see you on Monday. Today is my last day for three weeks.' Joanna asked her.

'Remind me where you're going.'

'Torremolinos, all-inclusive can't wait. I've bought two books to read while I'm away. I don't think they'll be a patch on your story. I told my husband about you; he said you'd had more than one lifetime, and it was better than anything on the telly.' Joanna haled her hand out and shook it.

'Thank you, that's lovely, so I didn't bore you then.' Rita picked up her briefcase and made her way up the hall. She reminded Joanna to think about a residential home. Joanna put her arms around and hugged her.

'Thank you for all you've done for me. au revoir,'
Three weeks later, Social Service Office.

'Look at the tan on you.' One of Rita's colleagues remarked as she walked in. She looked at the mountain of paperwork on her desk and sighed. Joanna's file was on top; it had a note saying called four times no answer.

'Yes, I did speak to the caretaker; he hadn't seen her; he said the block was half empty, just one big Giro drop.' Rita was angry at her colleague.

'She only had a weeks' worth of food; something must have happened.' Rita drove as fast as she could to the block. As usual, the lifts didn't work; walking along the passage to her flat, the door was open.

'Joanna, it's me, Rita.' There was no answer; walking up the hall, there was no sign of her. All her furniture and books were still in place, but the sideboard was missing. Rita started ringing all the local hospitals; there was no record of her.

'Do you have a photograph of her?' The police officer had completed the missing person form.

'No, I don't; what happens now?' Rita asked.

'Well, it'll be circulated in the area. Can I ask was this lady senile?'

'No, she was as sharp as a pin. She had a few health issues, but she could walk up two hundred steps.' Rita was becoming angry with him.

'You said her flat was intact apart from a sideboard; the front door was open when you visited her. Was anything else taken.'

'No.'

'There are two things that could have happened; she has lost her mind; we often find people wondering, or in the canal, second she's done a flit. That block is half empty. I don't think anyone left a forwarding address, and she might turn up yet. Is there anywhere she might go?'

Driving back to her office, she stopped her car, realising the only place would be Chinatown. The Chinatown Joanna knew had changed. On either side of the road were restaurants. Zhang Whi's laundry was now a restaurant; the sign in the window said 'All you can eat buffet three pounds.' Another poster said closed. She imagined Joanna going to the laundry the first time than telling Zhang Whi she'd killed Autile. Further down the street, some of the buildings were modern rebuilt after the bombing; a new cake shop was on the old site the sign said 'Annchi Liu famous celebration cakes.' Hoping they would help find Joanna, she approached; two young boys were playing football outside, asking them.

'I wonder if you could help. I'm looking for an old lady; her name is Joanna Barlow.' They shook their heads. Further down the road was a small supermarket; every item from floor to ceiling had packaging in Chinese; she wondered what the ingredients were; there was a strong aroma of spices and sandalwood. Rita felt as if she was in another country. The young woman behind the counter smiled as Rita asked.

'I wonder if you could help me, I'm looking for an old lady. Her name is Joanna Barlow. She was well known around here many years ago; they called her the Shanghai Lady.' The woman's face became serious.

'I don't know who that is, why you look for this person.' Before she could explain, an older woman started shouting in Chinese; she sounded angry.

'My grandmother asks you to leave.' Rita apologised, stepping outside she was confronted by a man.

'You shouldn't come here asking questions; you need to go.' Rita had a sleepless night; why were they so hostile to her. She had to find what had happened to Joanna. The next morning Her supervisor studied her case notes.

'You've exhausted every possibility, but sometimes there's no answer. I want you to close the file for the time being; just concentrate on your workload. Until we hear something, there's nothing we can do. People go missing all the time.' Rita pleaded with him.

'I got to know her; she just wouldn't leave something has happened to her. Why? If someone broke in, why would they just take the sideboard? It doesn't make sense. It's as if she vanished into thin air.'

Christmas 1981 Liverpool.

There was an air of excitement in the office as the staff got ready for their Christmas night out. While putting on her makeup, Rita listened as her colleagues joked about the night ahead.

'I'm going to snog Mike out of finance.'

'Well, he's got new teeth now he won't chew your lip off.' They all fell about laughing. The supervisor called everyone into his office, opening two bottles of wine; he made a short speech thanking them all for working so hard through the year. One of Rita's colleagues asked her who the present was off as they made their way out. Confused, she asked.

'I don't know what you mean?' Pointing to her desk.

'That one.'

Her heart was pounding as she looked at a small package; the stamps were Chinese and postmark Shanghai. With her hands shaking, she opened it. Inside was a jewellery box, a diary and a letter. The office was empty as Rita paused for a moment, praying for some news of Joanna. Slowly she read the letter.

My Dear Rita

First, I must apologise for all the distress I have caused you. Please accept my heartfelt regret for not telling you about my plans. I was fearful that you would have stopped me. I knew I was dying; my one wish was to be with Mai. The first day you came to my flat I gave you a letter to post for me, the contents of that letter were the arrangements for me to travel to Hong Kong then onto Shanghai. Zhang Whi's grandson was to make this possible. Once I arrived in Hong Kong, they smuggled me across the border to Shanghai to stay with Mai's family and live out my final days. As I write this letter, filled with happiness, my life story will be complete as soon as I am with my love. I will never forget you and the kindness you gave me. Please accept this gift as a token of my gratitude. Monique gave this to me. I have always treasured it. It's a symbol of love that shows lovers the way—also one of the hair rings of hope. The diary is my love letter to Mai. I hope you find the joy of knowing Mai in its pages.

Au revoir
Joanna

Rita's sobbing echoed around the empty office as she opened the jewellery box to reveal a pendant; she ran her finger across the white kingfisher swooping down on its journey to show lovers the way.

Shanghai January 1981
They placed Joanna's body wrapped in white linen sheets at the front of the boat. Mai was born on the same one, and her brothers showed their bottoms to angry neighbours. Mai's family began rowing as they made their way up the Wusong river towards their ancestral village. With the light fading, lanterns were set alight, and prayers were said. Turning along a slow bend, they moved towards a small wooden jetty. Hundreds of people carrying lanterns lined the riverbank. A drumbeat followed by cymbals rhythmically echoed through the woods as they lifted her from the boat onto the shoulders of Mai's relations. The procession made its way through the village to a graveyard that overlooked the Wusong. Placing her body next to Mai's grave, a monk recited prayers to help her soul find peace and avoid the fate of a restless ghost. Joanna Barlow was wearing the white dress she wore on her big day out; on her right hand, the engagement ring Monique gave her, around her neck, the ribbon of Xiang Yu to

the great warrior and the lock of Mai's hair. She was then lowered to the ground next to her love. The mourners stood in quiet reflection as the monk said a few more prayers. Two figures stood unseen in the shadows. Linking each other walking along the riverbank in their big adventure clothes with matching umbrellas, they paused at the water's edge. If you listened, you'd hear their laughter carried on the wind A full moon reflected in the still darkness. Downriver a white kingfisher swoops across the water, making ripples as the moon shimmered; two souls gathered up in its wings, the kingfisher flew over the buildings on the Bund, making its way to the mountains beyond.

Liverpool Chinatown 1982
The waitress handed Rita and her partner the menu, and then remarked on her pendant.
'That's beautiful white kingfisher very lucky.' Rita smiled, replaying.
'A friend of mine gave it to me; it's very precious.' While her partner surveyed the menu, she couldn't take her eyes off the sideboard behind the reception desk. An ornately carved sideboard, its legs intricately carved dragons' feet, and the centre door displayed a frieze of a kingfisher with its wings wide swooping down. The finish was black lacquer with gold inlays. Framed photographs on the wall behind, a photo of an attractive middle-aged woman signed 'All my love Monique.' two well-dressed young women, one European and one Chinese, sat at a table smiling happy and in love.

The end

About the author

Born Everton, Liverpool 1950

Worked in Power Utilities then Social Care

Member of Merseyside Comedy Writers.

Credits: ITV Laugh Last Show (McWilson)

Regular guest speaker at interest groups and rotary clubs with The Liverpool Lecky Man, Confessions of a Meter Reader.

A passionate advocate for continuing education for older people.

Retired Company director, Training Local Communities CIC

Still lives in Liverpool with his wife Pauline both caring for people with complex needs.

www.ingramcontent.com/pod-product-compliance
Lightning Source LLC
Chambersburg PA
CBHW050244120526
44590CB00016B/2203